The
Sweeping Business

The
Sweeping
Business

*Developing entrepreneurial skills
for the collection of solid waste*

Mansoor Ali & Andrew Cotton

Water, Engineering and Development Centre
Loughborough University
2001

WEDC

Water, Engineering and Development Centre
Loughborough University
Leicestershire
LE11 3TU UK

This publication is also available online at:
http://www.lboro.ac.uk/wedc/publications/sb.htm

Ali, S.M. and Cotton, A.P. (2001)
The Sweeping Business:
Developing entrepreneurial skills for the collection of solid waste

WEDC, Loughborough University, UK.

ISBN Paperback 0 906055 85 7

This document is an output from a project funded by the UK
Department for International Development (DFID)
for the benefit of low-income countries.
The views expressed are not necessarily those of DFID.

Designed and produced at WEDC
Cover photograph: Mansoor Ali

About the authors

Dr Mansoor Ali is a Project/Programme Manager at WEDC. As a specialist in solid waste management for low and middle income countries, he has researched and published extensively. Some of his current research projects include 'Waste and Livelihoods, Micro-enterprise Development, Appropriate Landfilling and Recycling.

Dr Andrew Cotton is the Director of Urban Programmes WEDC. A specialist in urban infrastructure for low-income countries, some of his recent research includes micro-contracts, operation and maintenance, knowledge management and urban sanitation.

Acknowledgements

The following persons and organisations have made valuable contributions to this research:

Jenny Appleton	WEDC, Loughborough University
Jo Beall	London School of Econimcs
Kevin Tayler	GHK International, Research and Training
Rod Shaw	WEDC Loughborough University
Kay Davey	WEDC Loughborough University
Sue Cotton	Freelance Consultant, UK
Jeremy Colins	Freelance Consultant, UK
Shafi-ul-Azam Ahmed	WSP Bangladesh Office

Community Action Programme, Faisalabad, Pakistan
Sevanatha, NGO, Colombo, Sri Lanka
ICDDR, B, Dhaka, Bangladesh
Water and Sanitation Programme (WSP), Bangladesh
Sweepers of Pakistan, Bangladesh and Sri Lanka who spoke to us
Municipal supervisors in research locations

Contents

Acronyms

ABO	Area Based Organisation
CBO	Community Based Organisation
CDC	Community Development Council
CIDA	Canada International Development Agency
CMC	Colombo Municipal Corporation
DCC	Dhaka City Corporation
DFID	Department for International Development (UK Government)
FAUP	Faisalabad Area Upgrading Project (a DFID funded project)
FDA	Faisalabad Development Authority
ICDDR,B	International Centre for Diarrhoeal Disease and Research, Bangladesh
KMC	Karachi Metropolitan Corporation

Glossary

Activist	Someone who follows the line of vigorous action for a cause.
Bangalee	A person from Bangladesh.
Daily worker	Worker employed on a day-to-day basis.
Dastoori	Traditional payments from sweepers to supervisors.
Filth depot	Transfer point to store waste.
Katchi abadi	Squatter settlement.
Lac	Equal to 100,000 in number.
Marla	An area of about $25m^2$.
Micro-enterprise	A low capital intensive service delivery or production business, consisting of an individual or up to about 20 people. The organisations or individuals are assuming all the risks for the sake of profit.
Mohallah	A group of houses in the same area.
Waste picker	A person who makes a living by extracting valuable elements from waste and selling them.
Punchayat committee	A committee formed at the neighbourhood level to resolve minor conflicts.
Parchee	Written permission from sanitary inspector to sweeper.
Sui gas	Natural gas.
VIP road	Important road.
Ward	The administrative areas into which a city is split.
Ward Commissioner	Political representative of an administrative section of the city
Wigar	Assigning duties for absentees
FMC	Faisalabad Municipal Corporation
MPA	Member of Provincial Assembly
MPCO	Multi-purpose Community Organisation
Rs	Rupees, Currency of Pakistan
Tk	Taka, Currency of Bangladesh
UWEP	Urban Waste Expertise Program
WASA	Water And Sanitation Agency

Section 1

Introduction and background

This document presents the findings from Project R6540 *Micro-Enterprise Development for Primary Collection of Solid Waste* carried out by the authors as part of the Technology, Development and Research (TDR) Programme, Engineering Division, Department for International Development (DFID) of the British Government.

The purpose of this project is to identify, explore and disseminate findings about the development of micro-enterprise in primary waste collection, working from a thorough understanding of existing processes, and to locate them in a broader framework of private solutions to solid waste management. The aim of this document is to provide guidance for promoting small-scale enterprises for primary collection of solid waste. It aspires to demonstrate the range of different solutions, which are applicable primarily to South Asia and possibly more widely. The findings in this book will be of use to policymakers and professional staff of both municipal authorities and non-governmental organisations.

Primary collection is the collection of solid waste from households and its subsequent transportation to the transfer points. In low income countries this is usually done manually or using a hand or animal drawn cart. We adopt the term *micro enterprise* to refer to a low capital intensive service delivery or production business, consisting of an individual or up to about 20 persons either officially registered or operating informally in an area. The organisations or individuals are assuming all the risks for the sake of the profit. *Entrepreneurial skill* is the individual's capacity to carry out or arrange a piece of work to be done, and to take risks in the hope of making a profit. In the context of this project, the issue under discussion is the primary collection of solid waste.

1

Key issues

- Urban governments in many developing countries are facing serious problems with the management of solid waste. Primary collection is often considered as the citizens' responsibility, whereas the municipal service is responsible for storage and vehicular transportation. However, this varies from one city to another. Citizens perceive service quality as poor, municipal capacity is limited and costs are spiralling, often with no effective mechanisms for financing nor cost recovery. Two solutions to the problem are currently favoured: decentralised approaches and privatisation.

- Decentralised approaches include activities which are beyond the boundaries of the roles of government agencies and the large scale private sector, for example, promoting the role of non-government and community based organisations in waste management.

- Privatisation may be a viable option but proposals are often hurried, ill thought out, and based on imported models which assume an entirely different technical, financial and organisational framework. This approach overlooks both informal sector activities at street level and the potential for area-based and non-government organisations to take a role in the privatisation process.

- Most privatisation proposals promise an improved service and envisage that the increased costs will be borne by users. To date, there is very little evidence of this being successfully achieved; efforts to increase user charges are usually blocked by politicians.

- Since the privatisation of all or part of many municipal solid waste systems will take place in the coming years, there is a need to address privatisation mechanisms by involving those who are amongst the poorest and who would potentially be most disadvantaged by the changes. Development of micro-enterprise initiatives can build on existing practices, which have been identified, thereby offering real potential as a workable component of privatisation strategy.

In a number of cities in South Asia, municipal and private sweepers collect waste from houses for an agreed payment. This is known as a 'Sweepers Collection System'. This project investigates the possibilities of, and conditions necessary for, upgrading current sweeper collection systems micro-enterprises. Our hypothesis is that the involvement of existing sweepers and community groups will improve the efficiency of primary collection, sustain or increase sweepers' income, improve their working conditions and reduce municipal responsibility and expenditure. It will thereby alleviate socio-cultural disruption and mitigate against an increase in poverty and/or unemployment.

In summary

- This research examines the potential of micro-enterprises for providing effective primary waste collection services in urban areas. This includes services for the poorest sectors of the community, who live in areas that may currently be unattractive to independent service providers.

- The research also recognises that the sweepers who provide solid waste management services are themselves among the poorest and most disadvantaged groups in urban society. There is therefore good reason to develop services that benefit not only consumers but also the operatives who deliver them. A key issue is how to provide sweepers with suitable incentives to deliver an effective, reliable operation.

- In South Asia, the role of sweepers in solid waste management is a deep-rooted social phenomenon that transcends municipal structures. This should be recognised by any initiative to introduce or improve primary collection services.

About this document

Section 1 concerns about the manual itself, the background and scope of work;

Section 2 identifies some key issues in solid waste management and describes current methods of collection;

Section 3 briefly describes the cases, which have been analysed, and refers to information boxes in Annex 1, where a detailed narrative is provided for each case;

Section 4 discusses the main themes, which emerge from the cases;

Section 5 offers guidance to all those wishing to initiate or promote the development of micro-enterprise in the primary collection of solid waste. This is the key section of the manual, and is identified by tinted pages.

Methodology

The research is based on investigating existing forms of micro-enterprises in the current practices of primary collection and to explore how they could be improved. Multiple methods of data collection were used in order to acquire data and relevant information. Processes of enterprise development and the perspective of various groups involved were fully explored throughout the research. Data was collected primarily from the following sources:

- 90 interviews with male and female sweepers;

- 30 interviews with sanitary supervisors;

- 15 case studies of local initiatives;

- 4 local workshops with the groups involved; and,

- Sharing of interim findings with the international community through an electronic conference and feedback.

Summary findings

- Opportunities for enterprise development can be promoted by recognising and integrating informal micro-enterprises, which demonstrate some remarkable features.

- Entrepreneurial skill is an important factor in sustaining primary collection initiatives and should be considered as an integral part of the project design. Often, entrepreneurial skills are overlooked as larger and more organised systems are designed.

- Most of the organised initiatives are developed because of a certain demand. The demand is latent, until an activist or organisation gives it a voice.

- Small scale primary collection initiatives have a remarkable capacity to collect the users charges. The system provides greater transparency and control to the users of the services.

- Small scale primary collection systems have demonstrated an impressive ability to mobilise local finances.

Section 2

Solid waste management

Solid waste: the context

Municipal solid waste management involves the storage, collection, transportation and disposal of waste generated in the home, commercial premises and institutions. As such, it comprises a complex set of operations that take place on an enormous scale. The city of Karachi, for example, consists of 8 million people who together generate more than 5,000 tonnes of solid waste daily. The solid waste sector consumes 20% to 50% of municipal revenue; in India, it employs between three and six people per 1000 of the population while Karachi Metropolitan Corporation alone provides at least 20,000 jobs.

Better solid waste management is an important element in improving the urban environment. Apart from the aesthetic problems created by solid waste, uncollected solid waste rapidly putrefies in hot and humid climates, giving rise to noxious smells and polluting leachates, as well as providing breeding grounds for vermin, flies and, in the wet season, mosquitoes. Poor solid waste management can also lead to blocked drains and contaminated water supplies, causing environmental health risks and infrastructure deficiencies. Solid waste management comprises a whole range of activities involving the public sector, small-scale private enterprises and service users.

Whose responsibility is it?

Municipal corporations and councils are charged with the task of solid waste management; it is usually the Health Department, headed by a Doctor of Medicine, which has overall responsibility. The Engineering Department maintains the vehicle fleet, and may provide an input if service contracts involving the private sector are involved. Given the size, complexity and budget share, it remains surprising that dedicated solid waste management departments are very rare in municipal government.

What happens to municipal waste?

Many Southern Asian countries do not have a formal house to house collection system; householders either deposit their waste in a communal container, or leave it in small piles outside the house. Municipal sweepers takes it to a larger waste transfer point, from where it is lifted and transported to a disposal site, sometimes via another intermediate transfer point. The collection frequency of the waste tends to be daily, but can vary depending upon the resources available and the perceived importance of the locality in question.

What do sweepers do?

Municipal authorities in low-income countries employ a large number of male and female sweepers to perform the sweeping of streets. In a typical city of five million inhabitants the total number of sweepers could be in excess of 10,000. Around 80% of municipal expenditure on solid waste operations are on sweepers' salaries. Sweepers are among the poorest of the poor, vulnerable and from the so-called 'low classes'.

The municipal sweepers are organised into a system of 'beats' i.e. determined by length of street, and there is hierarchical supervision within the Health Department which is usually based around council/corporation Wards (the key functional unit in urban local government). Vehicle crews are under the overall control of the Transportation Officer, who assigns their pick up routes. Sweepers have established posts within the municipality, and appointments are often related to social group and family history. In many towns and cities, sweepers groups have formed strong unions. Although sweepers are relatively poor and carry out what is often regarded as demeaning work, they nevertheless hold prized positions. Certain beats are regarded as more remunerative, and there are unofficial systems in existence whereby access rights are informally traded between sweepers and supervisors.

Matters are further complicated by the fact that municipal sweepers enter into informal contracts with households for the removal of waste, some of which is sold on. Some households enter into agreements with private sweepers (i.e. persons not in the employment of the municipality) for cleaning and the removal of household waste. Municipal and self-employed (private) sweepers offer a waste collection service to the households for an agreed monthly or weekly payment. Tips, gifts and food items often supplement the payment. The service and payments are generally agreed between sweepers as service providers and households as users of the service.

Is there a system of waste recycling and reuse?

The composition of solid waste entering the municipal waste stream indicates that (in contrast to Europe and America) there is very little paper, plastic, glass or metal; it is mainly silt (from road sweeping) and organic vegetable matter. However, the valuable content of solid waste is an important resource, and as a result there exists a highly developed system of waste recovery, reuse and recycling which operates on a commercial basis. This is not a system which has been developed by the public sector, nor is it an environmental hobby; it is market based and market driven.

Itinerant waste buyers purchase recyclable items door-to-door from householders or their servants; this material is sold on to middle dealers who may specialise in certain types of waste. Finally, there are the waste reprocessors; in earlier work (Ali, 1996) we estimated that this 'informal' industry could provide employment for up to 40,000 people in Karachi (an important centre for waste reprocessing). On a smaller scale, there are particularly complex intra-household relationships involving women and domestic servants which have gender implications (Beall, 1997). There are also large numbers of waste pickers who are not part of the formal system and who make their living from picking out material for reuse/recycling from communal bins, transfer points and waste disposal sites. These people may come from very poor background.

Who is responsible for the service?

In the four cities studied in this research, solid waste management is the mandatory responsibility of city, municipal and metropolitan corporations. It is generally accepted that these institutions do not deliver an effective primary collection service for a variety of reasons:

- in many cities, formal municipal responsibility starts with street sweeping; the collection of household waste is excluded;

- most municipalities consider waste transportation to be their main responsibility;

- municipal institutions are poorly financed and have no mechanisms for cost recovery; and,

- links between the service provider and the users are weak with no systems for complaints and consultation.

Local enterprises: a response to poor municipal services

One response to the generally poor service provided by municipalities is the local initiatives to collect waste; rich and poor alike are prepared to pay for improved waste services. Area based organisations (ABOs) and Non-government organisations (NGOs) have played important roles here to promote some form of local enterprise. This may involve municipal sweepers being paid extra, local activists either facilitating or managing collection, or a small contractor providing local services. These systems are the focus of this document.

Whilst these may appear to be ad-hoc solutions, they provide many important lessons for future strategies to promote micro-enterprise development in solid waste management. Official programmes to improve solid waste management tend to be city-wide and top-down, and are coupled with official policy and procedures. Public initiatives, however, are usually small- scale, local and dynamic. There is nevertheless scope for integrating them with official services. The fundamental unit of local enterprises is the sweepers system:

What is the sweepers system?

The sweepers' clients are households that generate waste, and are most likely to need their waste collected privately when this service is not available through the local authority. The sweepers system provides an essential service of waste collection to a wide range of income groups and local commerce (for further details see Ali, 1997, Beall, 1997 and Streefland, 1978). Such systems are now an integral or emerging feature of cities in low-income countries and are extensive both in terms of coverage and cost recovery. In addition to those sweepers employed by the municipality, there exist private self-employed sweepers who earn their living by providing waste-related services to households. Sweepers are the fundamental unit of primary collection systems and quite a complex range of roles can be identified as follows:

1. Municipal sweepers as wage earners who are earning a regular income through permanent or temporary employment with the municipal corporation.

2. Municipal sweepers doing private work who earn a regular income through permanent or temporary employment with the municipal corporations but supplement it through private waste collection and other jobs.

3. Private sweepers as 'survivalists', without a municipal job, who work independently. Their involvement in primary collection is a form of micro-enterprise with little prospect of growth and expansion, and is taken up due to a failure to gain waged employment. It is thus a livelihood strategy adopted by those with few alternatives in the labour market but with knowledge of, and access to, work in primary collection through informal institutional links and a network of reciprocity within sweeper communities.

4. Municipal and private sweepers as emerging entrepreneurs. In this case, sweepers have extensive networks of trust and reciprocity with households or community organisations and exploit them to ensure exclusive access to private work in primary collection for themselves, their family members and paid workers (or sub-contractors) known to them.

5. Municipal supervisors as emerging entrepreneurs, who give permission to and often manage and facilitate private work by municipal sweepers in return for payment (Boxes 26 to 28).

Types (2) to (4) in the preceding description are fundamental units of micro-enterprise from the perspective of sweepers themselves. Enterprise here is simply private work, whether combined with, or exclusive to, other paid work. It differs from paid employment, however, in several ways:

■ sweepers 'market' themselves to users;

■ sweepers negotiate their wages, which are not fixed;

■ they function as owner, manager and labourer;

■ they have full discretion to refuse work, take new work and sub-contract;

■ they manage both the inputs and outputs of the service;

■ there are elements of uncertainty in common with all small micro-enterprises; and,

■ there is evidence of personal investment such as buying a donkey cart for waste collection by sweepers.

Section 3

Range of enterprises

The findings of this research are based on a number of case studies. The case study material is presented as a series of boxes comprising a *narrative*, which describes the pertinent facts of the situation, and a corresponding *commentary*, which draws out significant points to be used as the basis for the discussion and guidelines. The narrative information is presented in some detail. As this requires considerable space, the boxes are located in Annexe 1:

■ Boxes 1 to 9 describe area-based systems in Pakistan;

■ Boxes 10 to 16 describe area-based systems in Bangladesh;

■ Boxes 17 to 25 present summary findings from interviews with municipal and private sweepers;

■ Boxes 26 and 27 present summary findings from interviews with municipal sanitary inspectors; and,

■ Boxes 28 and 29 present the key points arising from workshops with sanitary inspectors and supervisors.

Area-based systems in Pakistan (Boxes 1-9)

The research examined eight initiatives in Faisalabad, all involving ABOs and one initiative in Karachi involving an activist. Of those operating in Faisalabad, five are registered with the Social Welfare Department, one is actively considering registration and two are unregistered. An incentive for registering may be the small grants that may become available, although in one case a service provider with whom the NGO was negotiating required it. None of the ABOs specialises in solid waste management; some were formed for welfare activities while others provide vocational training. All, however, are involved in service provision, either directly or by lobbying the authorities, and operate in relatively middle income areas.

11

Summary of findings for Boxes 1 to 9 on area based systems in Pakistan

- Most of the area based organisations in the study operate a number of activities and primary collection of solid waste is one of these.

- There are two common approaches adopted to establish a system for the primary collection of solid waste.

1. To act as pressure group and procure additional staff from the municipal corporation.
2. To introduce private or municipal sweepers to the area, for an agreed monthly payment to the municipal staff.

In practice, both approaches result in some form of additional payment to sustain the sweepers.

- Those groups that operate with a defined contract between various parties run more sustainable programmes, for example, Liaquat Town Welfare Society (see Box 3).

- Primary collection of solid waste is not a high priority compared with other basic services such as water and sanitation if not available. Consequently, the markets for micro-enterprises are quite restricted for infrastructure deprived areas.

- Registration of the organisation with the government department concerned enhances the overall credibility, as perceived by organisations themselves.

- There is always scope available for external support agencies to promote the community-based initiatives.

- A summary of the solid waste management initiatives of different area based organizations in Faisalabad and Karachi could be summarized as follows:

Name of organization	Area	Description of activity	Financial transaction
Noor-ul-Amin Box 1.	Millat Road, Faisalabad.	Additional staff from FMC, monitoring their work, direct liaison with FMC head office.	No prescribed method of payment. Sweepers get some money as tips on festivals days and other occasions.
Muslim Town Welfare Box 2.	Muslim Town, Faisalabad.	Arranged private sweepers when the area was outside the municipal limits. Later received municipal services, as the area was included in the municipal boundaries. With both systems, households pay regular amounts to sweepers.	Households pay a monthly charge to the society.
Liaquat Town Welfare Box 3.	Liaquat Town, Faisalabad.	Introduction and negotiation with four additional sweepers to the area. Residents asked to pay a regular amount to sweepers. Involved more than 600 houses. Ensured payments from residents and proper work from sweepers. Prescribed method to dismiss sweepers or punish defaulting residents.	Rs 20 per month per house for the primary collection service.
M.A. Jinnah Development Box 4.	Shadab Colony, Faisalabad.	Introduction and negotiation with one private and then one municipal sweeper. Residents asked to pay a regular amount. Involved more than 100 houses. Loan to sweeper to buy a	Sweeper charge Rs 20 per month per house for the primary collection service. Sweepers pay 25% to M.A.

Name of organization	Area	Description of activity	Financial transaction
		donkey cart. Organising cleanliness campaigns. Social pressure on defaulters.	Jinnah for the community works.
Sulemaina Welfare Box 5.	Fat-he-Abad, Faisalabad.	Additional sweepers from FMC for the area and transfer of sweepers who were not attending the area. Payment of Rs 2 per week per house to sweepers.	Rs 2 per week directly to municipal sweepers.
Ayub Welfare Box 6.	Ayub Colony, Faisalabad.	Checking regularity of FMC sweepers. Interested in doing further work.	Some houses pay to sweepers Rs 3 per house per week.
Green Peace Welfare Box 7.	Firdous Colony, Faisalabad.	An additional seven sweepers for the area from FMC. They are allowed to use one Marla of land from Ayub Research Institute in return of waste (as fertilizer) for the institute.	Rs 3 per house per week.
New Public Welfare Box 8.	Saifabad, Faisalabad.	Introduction and negotiation with one private sweeper. Ask residents to pay Rs 10 per month per house to the sweeper.	Rs 10 per house per month to the sweeper.
Suzuki System Box 9.	F. B. Area, Karachi.	A politician introduced a house to house collection system using Suzuki vans. The programme covered 1000 houses. The municipal sweepers were asked to do street sweeping only.	Rs 15 per house per month was fixed, which was increased to Rs 25 after five years of operation.

Note: £ 1 @ Rs 75 in 1998

Area-based systems in Bangladesh (Boxes 10-16)

Different types of schemes have been studied in Dhaka, two schemes are run by activists, one by a ward commissioner, two by ABOs and two by NGOs. The ward commissioner who originated the service in Ward 36 acted on his own initiative and could be classed as an activist, albeit with a political role. The ABO-managed systems were inspired by discussions with the Environmental Health Programme of ICDDR.B, a Dhaka-based NGO. Both NGOs (Action Aid and Gram Shampad Unnayan Kendra) started their activities close to their offices in response to their perception of local needs. Action Aid is now trying to transfer the operation to local residents while Gram Shampad Unnayan Kendra plans to expand into other areas while maintaining responsibility for management of the services.

Only two of the initiatives serve low-income areas while one has a mixture of low- and middle-income residents. The remaining four areas could be described as middle- or lower- middle-income.

Summary of findings for Boxes 10 to 16 on area based systems in Bangladesh

■ Most of the area based organisations run primary collection of solid waste as one of their main activities.

■ There are three approaches adopted to establish a system for the primary collection of solid waste.

1. To introduce private or municipal sweepers in the area, for an agreed monthly payment.

2. To operate as a small enterprise collecting waste from 200 to 1000 houses and employing sweepers.

3. To monitor and modify the municipal sweepers system at the ward level.

It is generally accepted that some form of payment to sweepers is necessary in order to retain them. The general findings from the case studies in Dhaka are as follows:

■ The most commonly known programme in the city is the one which operates like a micro-enterprise (see box 14) in a middle income area. The programme was also regularly shown on the local television and considered as a model for other areas.

■ Primary collection of solid waste is becoming a high priority in the areas where residents have already acquired other services and infrastructure. The scope for primary collection programmes and micro-enterprises is increasing.

■ There is always scope for the external support agencies to underpin community-based initiatives. Some programmes in Dhaka have links with Dhaka City Corporation and with external donors.

■ There are indications that the transfer of knowledge, technology and learning is taking place from one programme to another.

■ Solid waste management initiatives of different area based organizations in Dhaka could be summarized as follows:

Box no.	Starting year	Houses involved initially	Houses involved now	Who initiated the programme	Current programme	Mode of payments
10	1994	250	250	The programme was initiated by an NGO, Gram Shampad Unnayan Kendra.	The programme operates near Green road area. A team of two sweepers and a waste picker collect waste from 250 houses. About 10 to 15% of the dwellers do not pay their service charges. One sweeper gets Tk 2500, another gets 1000 and the waste picker gets 300 per month.	A monthly fee of Tk 5 was fixed in the beginning, which has now been increased to Tk 20.

Box no.	Starting year	Houses involved initially	Houses involved now	Who initiated the programme	Current programme	Mode of payments
11	1995	39	39	The neighbour-hood commit-tee formed by ICDDR, B.	They ask DCC sweepers to attend the area regularly and collect waste from the houses. Removal of dustbins from the area with the help of the Ward Commissioner.	There is no payment to the sweepers, although there is now a neighbour-hood co-operative society.
12	1995	400	400	The local club formed in 1965, equiv-alent to a ABO. The programme operates in Jigatoal area, probably a low income area of Dhaka.	Two private sweepers, one male and one female, hired to pick-up waste from the doors. The sweepers collect money using a register and deposit it to the club. Each sweeper gets Tk 3000 as the monthly income, plus Tk 500 bonus once a year.	Each house pays a monthly service charge of Tk 20 per month.
13	1995	N/A	N/A	An elected Ward Commissioner initiated the programme in Ward 36.	The waste is collected from houses using 12 vans with 12 sweepers.	There is no charge for the service, although residents sometimes pay Tk 5 to 10 per month as tips to sweepers.
14	1987	250	750	The programme was initiated and is presently managed by Mr Mahbub Ahsan a	The programme operates in Kolabaghan, a middle income area of Dhaka. Two tricycles are used each	Tk 10 per house per month was initially charged, and was increased to Tk 15 in 1996. A money collector collects the money.

Box no.	Starting year	Houses involved initially	Houses involved now	Who initiated the programme	Current programme	Mode of payments
				resident of the same area. He invested capital himself and pays the salaries.	with 3 sweepers. All the sweepers are either municipal sweepers or their relatives. Dhaka City Corporation is positive about the programme. Each sweeper gets Tk 1200 per month from Mr Mahbub Ahsan.	
15	1997	963	963	The programme was initiated by an international NGO, Action Aid.	The programme is designed on the principles similar to Box 14. The waste is collected from 552 middle income and 411 slum dwellers. Slum dwellers get a free service.	The supervisor appointed by Action Aid goes house to house and collects money for Action Aid. Salaries are paid by Action Aid.
16	1996	100	100	The programme was initiated by Perveen, a female activist in the same area.	The programme operates in Charaon Nagar, a low-income area in Dhaka. Sweeper collects waste from 100 houses and takes it to the transfer point.	A payment of Tk 10 per month per house directly to the sweeper.

Section 4

Lessons learned

The purpose of this section is to draw together the lessons which have been learned from the wide range of case studies. The findings have been grouped into the following sections.

- Different systems for primary waste collection.

- Individual-based initiatives.

- Organised local initiatives.

- Roles, responsibilities and perceptions.

- Who initiates the demand?

- Whose enterprise?

- Who pays whom?

- Who finances the system?

- Is it profitable?

- What could be the municipal role?

- Concluding remarks.

Reference is made throughout to the Boxes in Annexe 1 which detail the individual cases.

Different systems for primary waste collection

We have found that there are two broad categories of the systems around which local initiatives are based:

- those based around agreements between householders and sweepers on a purely individual basis (see Boxes 17 to 24); and

- organised local initiatives which involve an Area-Based Organisation (ABO) facilitating or managing the relationship between households and sweepers or those which involve small scale local contractors (Boxes 9 and 14).

We can now consider these operational systems in more detail.

Individual-based initiatives

In this system, we can identify individual waste collectors as the fundamental unit of micro-enterprise for primary collection. Municipal and private sweepers offer household collection services for an agreed payment; we refer to this as the 'sweeper system'.

Municipal sweepers need permission from their supervisors to perform this private work and in return agree to pay them a proportion of their earnings (Boxes 17 to 24). A further agreement is made between fellow sweepers that they will not compete with each other by offering services in each other's territory; rights to private work may also be exchanged or bought with cash or favours. In summary, the sweeper system is based on a set of three verbal agreements:

- between sweeper and household;

- between sweeper and supervisor (if s/he is a municipal sweeper); and,

- between sweeper and fellow sweepers.

Advantages of the sweeper system include:

- simple and flexible to carry out;

- minimal overheads;

- direct benefits flow to the service providers who are amongst the poorest in society;

- users have power to hire and fire the service provider based on performance criteria; and

- the price for the service is based on users willingness to pay.

The sweeper system does have several disadvantages:

- as it is market-based, the poor are less able to pay the costs and the services do not often extend into low-income areas;

- from the perspective of city managers, there are problems in regulating the service, particularly in terms of lack of control over sweepers performance of their designated duties for the municipality; sweepers may and do perform private work when they should be carrying out municipal duties;

- in practice, there is less competition to provide a better, lower cost and more reliable service than might be supposed due to the informal agreements between sweepers;

- a further consequence of this is that users have less control over their sweepers; organising them into local user groups is one way of overcoming this.

Organised local initiatives

This term refers to a broad category of micro-enterprises initiated by households or entrepreneurs using municipal and/or private sweepers for primary collection. These arise when users organise themselves collectively to hire a private or municipal sweeper to collect their waste. We have found examples of such schemes initiated and managed by private individuals, municipal councillors and community based organisations (CBOs). Their motivation, organisational structure, mode of cost recovery and links with municipal institutions vary widely.

We can usefully categorise these systems into three groups:

- area-based systems in which individual householders pay sweepers;

- area-based systems in which the sweeper is paid centrally by the local organisation; and,

- small-scale local contractors who organise service delivery and collection of payments.

These are described in more detail below.

Area-based system which pays sweepers individually

Initiating the system. A group of households or a local activist decides to improve the waste collection system in their area by hiring a waste collector, introducing him/her to other households and fixing a minimum collection fee. Households pay sweepers directly. The activist or group may initiate the activity because of a perceived need or as a result of a community awareness-raising campaign from an outside agency (Box 1, 3, 5, 7, 8 and 16).

Sustaining the system. The local group or activist manages the system and sustains it through regular collection and payments. The sweepers' interest is the certainty of a regular group of customers and regular, known payments. A social obligation to pay arises from collective action and any defaulters are reported to the activist or group.

Implications for micro-enterprise development. This system is significant in several ways:

■ it shows the beginnings of a positive change in public attitude, in that users decide to act together rather than waiting for government to come and do the work; this opens up the potential for micro-enterprise in primary collection, albeit in a totally unregulated market;

■ users have a direct role in performance monitoring; official initiatives often overlook this important task;

■ if the system is introduced in areas previously without service, users can see a definite impact through a cleaner and healthier local environment;

■ sweepers have a comparatively secure, emerging market for their service; the assurance of regular minimum payments is an added incentive, and direct payment by households leaves room for the negotiation of higher rates and charges for additional work, which sweepers often carry out;

■ an important consequence of a more secure market is that sweepers are more willing to invest in the purchase of equipment such as simple tools and carts;

■ as the houses are located in one neighbourhood, sweepers do not have to collect waste from scattered locations which minimises unproductive travel time; and,

■ relationships of trust are developed which ensure co-operation in developing an effective service and a more secure livelihood.

Area-based system which pays sweepers collectively

Initiating the system. A group of households or an activist decides to introduce or improve a collection service in their area by hiring sweepers, introducing them to other households and fixing a minimum fee. The important distinction here is that the user group rather than the individual householders pay the salary of the sweepers. Some expenses such as buying equipment and paying for simple repairs are also borne by the organisers who perform this work on a voluntary or non-profit basis, but may receive support from external agencies (Box 1, 3, 5, 7, 8 and 16). The activist may be the elected representative for the area (Box 9 and 13) and may decide not to charge fees but to use government funds instead.

Sustaining the system. As with the previous system, the householders pay the fee to the organising group and the sweepers receive a fixed salary from the group. The responsibility for handling defaulters now rests with the local organisation rather than the individual sweepers.

Implications for micro-enterprise development. There are important additional implications to those described above for the area-based systems, which pay sweepers individually:

■ monitoring of the system further develops since the user group both facilitates the system and undertakes some financial control (Boxes 4, 10, 12, 15);

■ the scheme becomes closer to a 'paid labour' situation rather than a sweepers' enterprise; this may not be ideal from the sweepers' point of view as they lose the benefits of direct negotiation with households; however, they still have some opportunities for additional work and tips;

■ sweepers are usually reluctant to invest in the system as the risks are higher and ownership of the system is divided; the need for the user organisation to invest is therefore important; and,

■ the organising group sometimes keeps a share of the income as 'savings'; however, it may subsequently be reluctant to invest the money in the system and looks instead for external sources of funding.

Small-scale contractors

Initiating the system. An individual or contractor starts a waste collection programme as a business. They employ sweepers, introduce them to the households and charge fixed collection fees. The contractor pays the sweepers' salaries plus all capital and running costs, and tries to make a profit (Boxes 9 and 14). Sometimes the profit incentive may be combined with an interest in cleaning the area and gaining local recognition.

Sustaining the system. The system is driven by the profit incentive and survives through its ability to recover costs and generate a cash surplus for the contractor/entrepreneur.

Implications for micro-enterprise development. The implications are the same as for the previous area based systems, especially in terms of willingness to pay and user acceptance. These amount to a positive environment in which the micro-enterprise can develop. In addition:

■ the role of entrepreneur changes from sweeper to a comparatively larger scale contractor. The sweeper's role becomes that of salaried employee;

■ these systems operate on a relatively large scale: typically 500 to 1000 households in the cities studied;

■ the entrepreneur usually keeps operations at a level which can be managed individually, without external support or interference; and,

■ as the contract expands and sweepers again become labourers, some features of the sweeper system may reappear.

Roles, responsibilities and perceptions

Within these different organisational systems, understanding the roles, responsibilities and perceptions of different stakeholders gives additional insight into the way in which the system operates and the potential for further development. Here we use the term 'intermediaries' to describe local groups including ABOs, CBOs and NGOs.

Waste collectors

Our interviews with municipal sweepers revealed that they value their present jobs and would be reluctant to become micro-entrepreneurs, especially where they have not seen any examples to inspire them. Job security is seen as a major benefit of municipal employment, especially when other opportunities are few and uncertain. During the fieldwork, sweepers were asked their views on four hypothetical work options (Box 25):

■ to continue working in the municipal system;

■ to work for a private contractor;

■ to form their own micro-enterprises; and

■ to work with CBOs.

The majority interviewed wished to continue under the present municipal system, presumably because this maximises their benefits through a guaranteed salary and pension entitlement with the opportunity to top this up through private work. They also perceive benefits in collaborating with local organisations and micro-enterprises to earn an additional income. This suggests that any model of micro-enterprise built around sweepers should:

■ retain sweepers' job security through a basic guaranteed income; and

■ legalise additional earnings from private work.

The inherent problem with this is that it takes no account of how well sweepers perform their municipal duties. We can conjecture that there would be a lot of resistance to performance monitoring of these public duties. Nevertheless, a monitoring system needs to be negotiated to ensure that sweepers do not devote their entire time to private activities whilst still drawing their salary from the public purse.

Emerging micro-enterprises in primary waste collection can provide important livelihood opportunities for private sweepers who have no municipal job.

Intermediaries and waste collectors

From the point of view of a waste collector, the benefits of involving intermediaries such as ABOs or local NGOs include provision of a ready-made client group and the chance to progress from open competition for informal contracts with householders to a more formal contract with a group. This should reduce duplication of collectors' efforts and create a clearer demand for improved secondary storage and collection of waste.

Perceived disadvantages for waste collectors include lower income compared with private arrangements and possibly less autonomy; dependency on one small organisation could make them vulnerable to the risk of unemployment. Even though the income may not be enough on its own to support a family, waste collectors would probably be worse off without the involvement of local organisations. Generally, there is no evidence that the involvement of local activists, organisations and politicians reduces the income of waste collectors and some indication that it both increases it and makes it more stable.

Intermediaries and users
From the perspective of the users, reliability of the service is paramount and the involvement of intermediaries would undoubtedly be welcome as a means of guaranteeing this. Other advantages might include fixed fees and easier negotiation of charges for additional work.

Intermediaries can also pursue social goals such as employment creation and inclusion of the poorest members of the community; they are generally more effective in this than are municipalities. However, the picture is mixed: studies in Indonesia found that waste collectors are often hired from within the locality where waste is collected. By contrast, in South Asia, social issues are rarely considered important as waste collectors usually come from different social groups than the service users.

Intermediaries and Municipalities
Our analysis suggests that the involvement of intermediaries can also offer benefits to municipal government; this in turn may encourage the latter to respond positively to the idea of micro-enterprise in local collection services. Municipal systems in South Asia rarely involve service users in decision making; the only formal mechanism of contact between citizens and the municipality is through the Ward Commissioner who is usually responsible for neighbourhood solid waste services. Intermediaries provide an important additional means of bringing citizens concerns to the authorities. From the municipal viewpoint, the involvement of intermediaries could:

■ ensure that the service provides what users want; this can be achieved wherever users make regular payments for a collection service and are fully involved in specifying the level of service for which they are willing to pay;

■ reduce the need for public services at local level; and,

■ transfer some costs from the public to the private sector.

Whilst the latter two are less common, the case studies from Faisalabad and Dhaka do illustrate that this is possible. In both cases, intermediaries have introduced collection services in areas that were previously unserved. They, and in some cases the micro-entrepreneurs with whom they work, are providing management and financial resources that would otherwise be required from government or its agents. The position is less clear when local organisations use municipal sweepers but even here some reduction in management costs would be expected. We found that the best-managed services can cover the cost of primary collection, including management costs, with something left over for other purposes (Boxes 4 and 14).

The obvious disadvantages from the municipal perspective are the uncertainties inherent in micro-enterprise and possible competition with existing services run through councillors and Ward Commissioners. Services operated by Gram Shampad Unnayan in Dhaka, for example, are reportedly making a small loss because some householders do not pay their service charges; this casts doubt upon the long-term viability of the scheme. Furthermore, services dependent on activists appear less reliable than those supported by organisations. Nevertheless, all mediated activities are arguably more reliable than those undertaken directly by sweepers (Box 10).

We have identified three important sub groups of stakeholders within the municipal context and the 'municipal perspective' will therefore differ depending on which sub group is consulted, namely:

■ municipal officers in charge of the service and taking instructions from the mayor or administrator, conveying those to field officers (sanitary inspectors) and carrying out random checks for monitoring;

■ sanitary inspectors as field officers, managing an area such as an electoral ward; and

■ councillors as public representatives and the only link between users and the municipality.

Who initiates the demand?

Residents in response to the lack of an adequate service initiate most local systems for primary collection. The cases suggest that demand for a service often exists but that it is latent; it needs an activist or organisation to give it voice and bring the service into being. The activist may have a private agenda and may not consult residents very much at the planning stage. As long as the service provides what people want, this does not seem to matter; most users will pay.

Having said this, demand alone cannot guarantee sustainability. A weakness of these systems is that whilst they are mostly independent initiatives, they rely on provision of a secondary collection service if (as is usually the case) local disposal is not possible. Without some degree of municipal support, therefore, an initiative may not be sustainable.

Long term success also depends on user confidence in the service provider. The larger the operation, the greater the managerial demands and the sums of money changing hands. A minimum degree of operational competence and financial transparency is needed if customer confidence is to be retained.

Whose enterprise?

Entrepreneurial skill of sweepers and small-scale contractors is an important factor in sustaining these systems and should be encouraged from the start. As long as the system is small, sweepers display many entrepreneurial characteristics in that they accept some financial risk, have only partial security and negotiate directly with customers. As the size of the operation expands, it is the activist or contractor who takes on this role, with the sweeper becoming a regular employee.

An important lesson here is that a strategy to assist the poorest of the poor should focus on small initiatives, although this could create management problems for local authorities with no experience nor training in managing small units. It could be seen as an 'additional work'. Caution is in any case needed before developing a strategy based on micro-enterprise. By definition, a greater degree of enterprise means greater financial risk, and although this could result in higher income, the research shows that security is highly valued by sweepers – hardly surprising given their meagre income and low social status. In other words, it would be wrong to assume that sweepers want to become entrepreneurs, straightaway. As discussed earlier, for them the optimum situation appears to be one whereby they have a secure basic income but can supplement it by negotiating additional work with householders, to the benefit of both sweeper and the local environment.

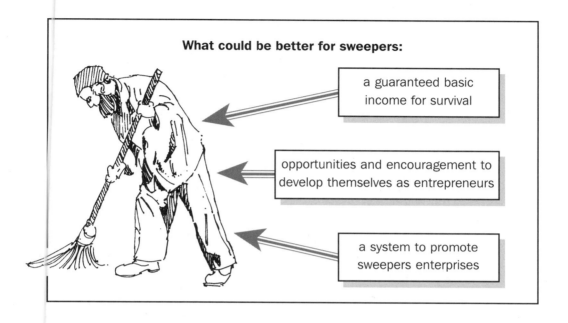

What could be better for sweepers:

a guaranteed basic income for survival

opportunities and encouragement to develop themselves as entrepreneurs

a system to promote sweepers enterprises

Who pays whom?

The ability to collect money owed is the fundamental factor in sustaining any business. In the cases investigated, the service provider was able to collect money from over 90% of those using the service; this compares very favourably with the collection efficiency for municipal taxes which is 40-60% in the cities studied. The reasons for this remarkable achievement are:

■ users pay someone they know;

■ users can see how their money is being spent; and

■ users can withhold payment if not satisfied with the service.

This is a major strength of small-scale enterprises in primary collection; indeed the sweeper system has been accepted by residents for many years. This provides a strong case for the promotion of small schemes serving 200 to 1000 houses. It does not detract from the need for secondary collection and disposal services, which require more centralised management and cost recovery systems.

Who finances the system?

In all cases, there was evidence of finance being mobilised locally. The sources included investment by small-scale contractors; collections made by user groups; accessing municipal funds; and, funding by the local elected representative. Funds from institutional sources were only provided to comparatively large schemes. This raises the question as to how small initiatives which may not be eligible for loans from commercial banks can raise capital finance for the purchase of equipment and tools. This could be particularly difficult when attempting to introduce services into low-income areas where cost recovery is less assured.

NGOs could play a key role here by acting as guarantor to lenders on behalf of the activist group, or by providing loans at a concessionary rate of interest. This reduces the burden of risk from both lender and micro-entrepreneur. Alternatively, they could provide the hardware itself and recover the cost in instalments, perhaps after a period of grace, during which the scheme builds up its customer base. NGOs can also play an important capacity building role to develop the financial and managerial skills needed to run an operation effectively. The larger the operation, the greater these demands will be.

Even with NGO support, many uncertainties surround the promotion of primary collection services as micro-enterprises. Widespread replication of small schemes is unlikely to take off unless they can demonstrate a rate of return which makes them viable businesses providing real jobs with acceptable levels of income rather than 'community services'. At present, many schemes are in the latter category, with a tendency to seek subsidies through donor support rather than operating on truly commercial lines.

Is it profitable to run an enterprise?

It proved difficult to obtain financial details for the cases studied. Systems operated by small contractors tend to make a profit; in Dhaka, for example, local initiatives make a profit of 10 –20 %. Even with a reliable customer base, there are constraints on the amount of profit that can reasonably be made from such schemes:

- fees are usually determined by user willingness to pay rather than an analysis of the income needed to make an operating surplus;

- some NGOs and donors are uncomfortable with the principle of a community service making a profit;

■ where the concept of privatised services is accepted by government and donors, it is usually coupled with regulations to limit the amount of profit that can be made; however there is no evidence that this has yet filtered down to these small local initiatives; and,

■ cost recovery is often achievable for small schemes dealing with primary collection only; it would be much harder to recover costs if a contribution were required towards the other steps in the solid waste management stream upon which these initiatives depend.

What could be the municipal role?

In all of the systems described previously, the role of municipal government is negligible; indeed the systems operate because municipal services are poor or non-existent. Most of the local initiatives operate in middle- to high-income settlements where households are willing to pay a user charge, which the entrepreneur perceives to be realistic in order to provide the service. A major challenge lies in finding ways to extend services to all income groups while preserving benefits to the entrepreneurs (including sweepers) who provide them. The financial ambitions of schemes in slum areas will have to be realistic; perhaps 'breaking even' could be a definition of success as it would at least enable some environmental improvement to be achieved.

A potential role for the municipality here could be in promoting schemes in areas that are currently unattractive to micro-entrepreneurs. This may not be easy, but they could try to create a conducive environment through both policy and operational support. This might include:

■ inviting competent NGOs into the area, collaborating with them closely and providing logistical support;

■ deploying more sweepers and encouraging them to make private arrangements with households (so that basic staff costs are covered from the municipal budget); this has to work hand-in-hand with a system for monitoring to ensure that sweepers actually perform the duties for which they are paid by the municipality;

■ ensuring reliable secondary collection; and,

■ getting elected representatives to help generate demand for the service.

A policy which recognises and endorses the sweeper system could be important for two reasons.

- Municipal support is vulnerable to the whims of individual managers or councillors who may offer staff or vehicles one month only to redeploy them the next when a new priority comes along. A formal policy could remove some of this instability and give more confidence to potential micro-entrepreneurs.

- Any municipal initiative to improve solid waste management may founder if it does not recognise the established informal arrangements under which sweepers already work. For example, the introduction of a large-scale private contractor may cause disruption and conflict if the municipality take no remedial action to compensate sweepers who already provide an informal service in the area. The best way forward may lie in incorporating the sweeper system into the new service.

If a municipality adopts a strategy to promote the widespread adoption of micro-enterprises for primary collection, it is important to develop a simple regulatory system, which contains minimum safeguards. For example:

- to set a framework for the operation of small schemes including rules (e.g. a prohibition on burning waste), roles, basic performance standards and possibly charge rates to create some consistency across the city;

- to establish a policy of encouraging small schemes rather than large-scale contracts for primary collection;

- to legalise the undertaking of private work by sweepers, subject to monitoring their performance of municipal duties;

- to co-ordinate links between the primary collection schemes and secondary collection, haulage and disposal which remain the responsibility of the municipality and its contractors; and

- to act as arbiter between competing schemes by deciding which group can operate where.

Such a regulatory system could be a municipal responsibility, as in Bangalore, India, where there are many NGOs and CBOs vying to run local initiatives. An agency has been established with representatives of both government and

NGOs. The difficulty with this proposal is that most municipalities in low-income countries are inexperienced and unskilled in regulating small enterprises.

Privatisation in Karachi

A pilot scheme to introduce a privatised solid waste management service (from primary collection to disposal) was launched in one zone of Karachi in 1998. After tendering, the contract was awarded to a local operator with modest local experience in the sector. This contractor had to supply all plant and equipment and deploy his own waste collectors, none of them from the former municipal workforce (this was in fact a condition of the contract). Shortly after the contract began it became apparent that the municipal corporation had not made adequate arrangements for the re-deployment of municipal sweepers, many of whom continued to provide a door-to-door service in the area.

Concluding remarks

Opportunities for enterprise development could be promoted by recognising sweepers' traditional roles and making them more secure. This role then could be gradually upgraded to sustainable micro-enterprises. In Colombo, where the research found comparatively effective official institutions with a credible experience of reaching the poor, sweepers accept the idea of micro-enterprise and talk of agreements with local organisations known as Community Development Councils (CDCs).

Encouraging the growth of informal micro-enterprises may seem an ad hôc and inadequate response to the needs of a large city. This may be so, but at the same time it is pragmatic. Nevertheless, the need for medium to long term planning must not be undermined. Municipalities are unable to provide primary collection services and small initiatives already exist; it therefore makes sense to develop conditions under which they can thrive to the benefit of the community.

At a local level, a micro-entrepreneur can manage the demand, the service, the labour and equipment necessary for its delivery. Such arrangements involve direct contact between micro-entrepreneurs and their customers and tend not to involve government.

In order to integrate existing enterprises into future privatisation strategies it is important to strengthen the roles of three principal actors: government, civil society and the enterprises themselves. Each has a different perspective that needs to be understood for the benefit of socially balanced solid waste management.

It is important to appreciate stakeholder perspectives and to incorporate them in future strategies for the promotion of micro-enterprise. This section has looked at the perspectives of three stakeholders but there may be other important groups in some situations.

Weaker groups among the stakeholders (e.g. sweepers) would prefer to continue in their existing situation, primarily to avoid the risks of entering an unknown system, but enterprise could be promoted via several routes. Our analysis suggests that the involvement of intermediaries has potential benefits for the users, providers and the agency responsible.

Section 5

Guidelines

Introduction

The purpose of this section is to provide guidance for improving primary solid waste collection in neighbourhoods through promotion of local small enterprises, ranging from individual entrepreneurs to small contractors.

The guidelines will be useful to those different groups who are likely to take the initiative in improving matters. These include:

- local activists in the area concerned;

- local resident groups;

- NGOs who are supporting local resident groups;

- local councillors and municipal officers wishing to improve the overall quality of service; and,

- local support staff of donor agencies who both plan and implement programmes.

These guidelines do not propose a step by step methodology leading to guaranteed success; we are dealing only with processes, local circumstances will dictate precise details. This section is structured around the range of possible activities which reflect the differing roles and responsibilities, that we have encountered. The guidelines are presented in a series of text boxes (Boxes G1 to G13). These include examples, which are drawn from the cases presented in Annexe 1.

35

Guidelines

The guidelines cover the following types of micro-enterprise development:

- developing the existing sweepers' system;

- promoting area-based systems through local organisations; and,

- promoting small-scale local contractors.

By adopting these approaches, it is possible to address the important objectives of improving local services and providing income generation and enterprise opportunities for marginalised groups of the urban poor.

The guidance, which focuses on relevant issues is based around the key points for programme preparation which are summarised in Box G1. As you work through the section you will be referred on to other Boxes which give more specific details on the relevant issues.

Box G1. Preparing for the programme

The following questions and issues need exploring when preparing a programme for improved solid waste collection.

- Is there sufficient interest amongst local residents to merit an improved system for local primary collection of solid waste; for example are some residents already paying for extra services?

- The need for an awareness raising programme should be considered (Box G2).

- Are the residents willing to pay for an improved service? Payments at the inception of the programme may be low, but may gradually increase once the service is shown to function well (Box G3).

- Are there existing local organisations, committees or NGOs who are prepared to take on responsibility as area organisers for primary waste collection? If not, are there individuals who are willing to come together to create an organisation in the area for this purpose ? (See Figure 5.1.)

Box G1. Preparing for the programme *(continued)*

- Are there municipal and private sweepers already operating in and around the neighbourhood? (Box G4.)

- Contact those sweepers or local contractors who are working in or near the neighbourhood and find out whether they are interested in being recruited. It is important to find out if there is any conflict between different groups of waste collectors (Box G4).

- Discuss the need for basic equipment including any special clothing required to protect operatives from possible hazards caused by handling waste (Box G5).

- Discuss how the start-up costs of the programme including equipment might be financed (Box G6).

- Contact the local ward office of the municipality to discuss the proposed programme with elected officials and public health officers in order to see how the municipal system can support the new programme (Box G7).

- Identify other constraints such as problems of local access (Box G8).

- Identify local transfer points for secondary collection (Box G7).

- Agree performance criteria for monitoring with the waste collectors/ contractor (Box G9).

- Agree the mechanism for registering complaints, for both service users and service providers (Box G10).

- Prepare a verbal or written contract so that each party is clear about its roles and responsibilities (Box G11).

- Monitor the service and make sure that the outcome is regularly communicated to both the service users and service providers (Box G9).

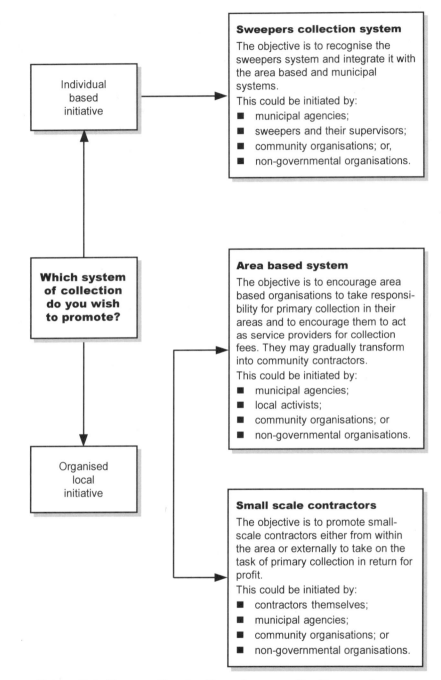

Sweepers collection system

The objective is to recognise the sweepers system and integrate it with the area based and municipal systems.

This could be initiated by:
- municipal agencies;
- sweepers and their supervisors;
- community organisations; or,
- non-governmental organisations.

Individual based initiative

Which system of collection do you wish to promote?

Area based system

The objective is to encourage area based organisations to take responsibility for primary collection in their areas and to encourage them to act as service providers for collection fees. They may gradually transform into community contractors.

This could be initiated by:
- municipal agencies;
- local activists;
- community organisations; or
- non-governmental organisations.

Organised local initiative

Small scale contractors

The objective is to promote small-scale contractors either from within the area or externally to take on the task of primary collection in return for profit.

This could be initiated by:
- contractors themselves;
- municipal agencies;
- community organisations; or
- non-governmental organisations.

Figure 5.1: Preparation for the primary collection programme through micro-enterprise development.

Guidelines

Box G2. Raising awareness

Problems

Householders often give low priority to improving solid waste collection services; unless they understand the problems and are actively looking for solutions, demand for improvements needs to be assessed and promoted through raising public awareness in order to:

- expand limited market opportunities for micro-entrepreneurs;

- create a stable demand to encourage entrepreneurs to build a business in the area; and,

- improve the local environment.

Guidance

Intermediaries (individuals and organisations) and municipalities can help create the conditions necessary for successful enterprise development by promoting public awareness of the need for better solid waste management. Emphasis could be given to the improvement of the local environment and health. The impact of poor solid waste management on other infrastructure is also important. Small entrepreneurs or community groups may not be able to fund large scale campaigns without the support of external funding agencies.

Approaches to raising awareness need to take into acount the scale and purpose of the campaign, the target group and the resources available:

- for small areas of less than 100 households, word of mouth may be effective i.e. an activist making personal contact with residents;

- for larger areas, residents' meetings and leafleting could be more appropriate, although meetings may attract low attendance if the priority for a collection service is low;

- for the purpose of developing replicable models, large-scale awareness campaigns through the media could be important. It appears, in fact, that few of the case study initiatives needed much effort in this area; several referred to awareness-raising but few needed to do very much;

- in many cases, it appears relatively easy to interest people in improved services once the possibility of providing them has arisen; the main task is then to publicise how effectively that service could be delivered rather than to raise awareness of the need for a service; and,

Box G2. Raising awareness *(continued)*

■ NGOs are more effective than CBOs in this area as they tend to have access to new ideas and can reach a wider audience; however, the example of EXNORA (Bangalore, India) suggests that a lead NGO supporting a network of affiliated CBOs can also be an effective institutional mechanism.

Some examples

In the four **Dhaka** case studies, the initiators of the services assumed that there would be a demand and this proved, on the whole, to be correct (see Boxes 15 and 16).

■ The Kashmiritola Lane committees received training on issues in waste disposal and health but did not, apparently, pass this on to the rest of the community (Box 11).

■ In Dhaka, televised information on the Kolabaghan programme led to a number of groups approaching the organiser (Box 14).

■ The need for primary waste collection in the Jigotal area was identified in a survey that may also have helped to raise community awareness (Box 12).

■ In Ward 36, the service was introduced by a local councillor following the failure of a system based on the use of dustbins which caused a nuisance. A leaflet was distributed informing people of the new collection system - a basic form of raising public awareness (Box 13).

Among the **Faisalabad** case studies there are further examples.

■ M.A. Jinnah Society in Shadab Colony felt the need to motivate people before starting their waste collection service. This was done through lane level meetings. A cleanliness campaign at the time the system was started may also have helped to raise its profile (Box 4).

■ The Liaqat Town Welfare Society conducted an area campaign promoting the benefits of the proposed waste management initiative. After this received an encouraging response, they circulated a one-page agreement whereupon 600 households gave a written undertaking to pay the proposed fee of Rs. 20 per month (Box 3).

■ The Sulemania Welfare Society provides an interesting example of lobbying the municipality to get piles of garbage removed and raising awareness among young people taking part in the exercise (Box 5).

Guidelines

Box G3. Sustainability and cost recovery

Problems

A primary collection programme can be sustained if there is enough demand, if users are willing to pay and providing that an entrepreneur is willing to continue the programme.

■ Full cost recovery is essential for the sustainability of all types of primary collection schemes. This includes operational costs, loan instalments for capital expenditure and savings for the replacement of equipment and vehicles.

■ Small systems tend to be sensitive to 'shocks'; even low levels of defaulting on payment threaten the survival of micro-enterprises.

Guidance

The following guidelines should be considered when planning for cost recovery.

■ There is a need to match willingness to pay with the estimated costs of operating the service. Whilst we can envisage an important role for NGOs and ABOs here, it is important that they themselves are competent to intervene in this area. This depends upon the perceived importance of the service, confidence in the provider, etc.

■ Ease of payment is essential for systems which involve an area based organisation; the service provider has to be paid a predictable amount regularly so that he knows what his cash flow will be.

■ Area based systems which collect payments from users have to have a transparent system of accounting, which regularly informs users of the income and expenditure position.

■ Users want to see the maximum possible spent on service delivery and the minimum on overheads.

■ NGOs and ABOs may be able to provide support to overcome financial shocks and get the initiative back on its feet.

■ For large operations including city-scale activities, cost recovery may be part of a regular municipal system for the collection of charges and any changes may require legal approval.

■ See also Guidance Box G6 , Financing.

Box G3. Sustainability and cost recovery *(continued)*

Some examples

The Suzuki system (Box 9) fixed a charge of Rs 15 per month per house in 1988. Two used Suzuki vans were purchased, one for Rs 20,000 and other for Rs 25,000, from the personal financing. The charges were collected directly by the programme organiser and raised to Rs 25 in 1994. The programme organiser instructed the collection crew to collect waste from all the houses, whether they were paying monthly charges or not. However, the programme soon expanded and gained popularity among residents; as a result, all 1000 houses in the area started paying the charges regularly. Residents felt that they got a reliable service for which they were willing to pay.

Box G4. Finding out about sweepers

Problems

Municipal and private sweepers are of key importance in primary collection; they are the 'occupational custodians' of waste related services and are amongst the most vulnerable employees in the waste business. It is extremely important to understand their stake in existing and future systems of waste collection. Any new initiative in primary waste collection may affect them; for example, if a local organisation initiates an awareness scheme, this may lead to increased demand. Sweepers from other areas may be attracted to fulfil this demand.

Guidance

Finding out about sweepers is an important part of the planning process. It may be useful to ascertain the following information.

- How many sweepers are attending the area?

- How many sweepers are municipal employees and how many are self employed?

- Are they already involved in providing a waste collection service for agreed payments by residents?

- Are there sweepers in nearby areas who would be interested in taking up work in the proposed waste collection service?

Examples

WEDC's 'Capacity Building Project', Citizen Guides have been produced for the cities of Karachi, Dhaka, Faisalabad and Colombo. One essential section of the guides gives details of the number of sweepers who are supposed to be covering a certain area and contact details for their supervisor's office. Such details were found to be extremely useful to community organisations in finding out more about sweepers. Information exchange mechanisms could be set up to share information about availability and reliability of both municipal and private sweepers.

Box G5. Technical support

Problems

Whilst the technology appropriate for primary collection of solid waste is relatively simple, the provision of technical advice may be beyond the competence of most activists and CBOs:

■ technology development is often a gradual process involving modification in response to local conditions;

■ maintenance systems also need to evolve once a service is in operation taking account of users' requirements; and,

■ micro-enterprises cannot afford to take risks with innovation.

Guidance

■ Examples of successful innovations need to be recorded. NGOs are generally better placed than ABOs to disseminate ideas but it is important that they have access to some form of grassroots organisation.

■ Where individuals have developed knowledge through previous experience, they can provide technical support to micro-entrepreneurs by providing or accessing technical advice on the choice and design of equipment and/or providing assistance with repairs and maintenance.

■ Occasionally, innovative design can play a vital role in initiating a service but the technology needs to be simple and intermediaries need to be prepared to modify designs to incorporate users' suggestions. Good designs could be a trigger to initiate the service. NGOs and municipal corporations could share the burden by testing innovative designs under similar conditions

Some examples

In Shadab Colony, Faisalabad, improved designs for donkey carts and handcarts have played a pivotal role in mobilising community resources (Box 4).

In Dhaka, technical innovations developed during the Kolabagan initiative were recorded and have been replicated elsewhere (Box 14).

Box G6. Financing

Problems

Potential entrepreneurs may be prevented from starting a solid waste collection service by lack of funds to buy simple but essential equipment such as a handcart or donkey cart. Finance is also necessary to overcome initial delays in user payment whilst the customer base is built up. Specific problems include:

- the low social and financial status of waste collectors which means that they are rarely able to provide the necessary guarantees required by banks; and,

- loans available from the informal sector tend to have high interest rates, which may deter new entrants to an apparently uncertain market.

Guidance

There is limited real scope for assisting individual sweepers who need to look to their own social and family networks for support. However, an area-based system which pays sweepers collectively (a type of user association), or which engages a small contractor could help by:

- purchasing the equipment then hiring it out to the micro-entrepreneur; or

- providing a loan at a reasonable rate of interest, perhaps using the equipment as security.

Some examples

- In Shadab Colony, Faisalabad, an ABO financed the purchase of an improved donkey cart by providing the waste collector with a loan which was repaid by monthly instalments (Box 4).

- In Kolabaghan, Dhaka a small contractor obtained money from his relatives to fund the initial purchase of equipment (Box 14).

- In Ward 36, Dhaka, rickshaw vans were purchased from municipal funds and financial aid from local industrialists (Box 13).

Guidelines

Box G7. Linking local collection to the municipal system

Problems

Waste collectors need to dispose of the waste which they have collected. The availability of transfer points and the provision of a reliable secondary collection system are extremely important for the successful operation of primary collection micro-enterprises. These are not always available, particularly in low-income congested areas and the secondary collection service by the municipality is often very poor. Consequently, uncontrolled dumping of collected waste on low-lying land is common. Ideally, the primary collection programmes should be fully integrated with municipal systems in all aspects.

Guidance

■ Activists and local organisations could lobby municipal government to provide extra transfer points; elected local representatives may also be mobilised to help.

■ Some municipalities are purchasing movable containers of 3 to 5 m³ for secondary transportation, which may be an option for the local transfer points.

■ Activists and local organisations can assist municipalities by identifying appropriate areas for secondary transfer points.

■ Investigate improving waste reduction and recycling programmes at source to reduce the scale of the problem.

Some examples

■ In Faisalabad, the Green Peace Welfare Society obtained a small patch of land (1 marla, or 25m²) from an agricultural research institute on the understanding that the waste would be available to the institute for fertiliser (See Box 7).

■ Also in Faisalabad, people in one neighbourhood of Chak 7 recently decided to introduce small communal containers instead of house-to-house collection. Interestingly these containers, though heavily promoted by professionals, are rarely acceptable to residents because of disagreements about their siting and fears that they will not be emptied. The Chak 7 experience provides an initial indication that the involvement of a local CBO may help to overcome this problem but the initiative is in its early stages and needs to be further monitored.

Box G8. Improving local access

Problems

Primary collection of solid waste is difficult in areas with poor local access. Handcarts, bicycle rickshaws and motor vehicles cannot be used where surfaces are uneven and rough; even donkey carts, which can tolerate some unevenness in road surfaces, cannot negotiate streets that have not at least been levelled. Poor road surfaces reduce operational efficiency and shorten the life of collection equipment. The condition of streets outside the local area can also hamper the movement of waste to transfer points. All these problems constrain the promotion of micro-enterprises.

Guidance

■ Local organisations could improve local streets for example, by raising funds from residents.

■ Activists and local organisations could lobby municipal government to upgrade local access and paving as part of general area upgrading rather than improvements specifically related to solid waste management.

■ Find out whether elected local representatives have funds for these general local improvements.

■ The selection of the equipment and vehicles could be made to suit the physical layout of the area.

Some examples

There are several examples from the FAUP in Faisalabad.

■ The first request to the FAUP by the M.A.Jinnah Society was for a scheme to improve the main Bazaar in Shadab colony. Although not essential to the operation of the service, the surfacing made access to the transfer points easier. Serious problems remained in less developed areas.

■ In Chak 7 a large pond obstructed a crossroads in the village centre; streets were also uneven and unsurfaced. Drainage of the pond was an early priority for the project. Completion of this scheme plus improvements to road surfacing funded through locally elected representatives improved the situation sufficiently for the ABO to introduce primary collection in some areas.

■ Pressure for the initial improvements by the local authority came from informal residents' groups rather than an ABO; this had positive results.

■ In Noor Pura, lane organisations have used the cost sharing arrangements offered by FAUP to construct sewers and at the same time provide a constant level to streets which were previously very rough and uneven. Donkey carts now have access to lanes where previously no service was possible.

Box G9. Monitoring the system

Problems

Performance monitoring is essential for effective operation of the system and important lessons can be learned from the past. The difficulty lies in developing a system which can be used with the minimum of effort; this should not be underestimated, otherwise the time and cost involved becomes prohibitive in relation to the scale of the primary collection scheme. The programme organisers must be fully convinced about the need for monitoring. The monitoring becomes more complex where municipal sweepers are involved because the monitoring system needs to take account of the fact that they are supposed to clean streets as part of their municipal duties.

Guidance

The level of performance expected has to be mutually agreed between the client (household or ABO) and the sweepers or contractor. This can be stated at the outset, but it is just as likely that changes will be negotiated over a period of time as it becomes more apparent how effectively the system is working and where the problems lie. At one level, the household monitors individual contracts between households and sweepers while disputes are resolved by direct negotiation.

Area based organisations are well placed to carry out monitoring of schemes for which they employ sweepers or small contractors. Small-scale operations tend to be closely monitored especially when the operator lives in the same area.

Where municipal sweepers operate, there is the potential to develop performance monitoring criteria which take account of their street cleaning responsibilities paid for by the municipality. This would benefit both the ABO and the municipality in terms of value for money, whilst affording the sweepers security plus the opportunity of earning additional income. We have not found any examples of this.

City systems are generally monitored through random checks and following residents' complaints.

Performance could be monitored using the following criteria:

- cleanliness of streets, assessed through visual checks and comparison with visual aids such as photographs of streets meeting the desired standard;

- cleanliness of transfer points, assessed through visual monitoring of waste accumulation and spread at various times of the day;

Box G9. Monitoring the system *(continued)*

■ number and frequency of complaints;

■ users' satisfaction survey (at least once a year);

■ regularity of payments by householders and ABOs to the sweepers and contractors; and,

■ regular checks on the state of equipment need to be carried out by the operator and brought to the attention of the party responsible for maintenance.

Some examples
Khulna Project, Bangladesh
Water and Sanitation Programme (WSP) in Bangladesh has set up a pilot project in Khulna, focusing on primary collection. Success and sustainability indicators were developed for the project, in association with WEDC and field tested in March, 2000. The indicators were developed, keeping in view various perspectives and could be used to monitor the project *for more details see WEDC's publication: Success and Sustainability Indicators.*

Box G10. Dealing with complaints

Problems

Traditional municipal waste management does not as a rule have a system whereby service users can register complaints for subsequent resolution. However, from the users' perspective, it is extremely important that their complaints are listened to and dealt with promptly. A complaint system, which is locally based, is an important element in the credibility of micro-enterprises in primary collection.

Guidance

■ A major advantage of small operations is their potential to deal with complaints locally and promptly. At this scale, systems can be very simple; they must be reliable and users need to know how they work, where they have to go and what they have to do to register a complaint.

■ It is logical to use area based organisations for registering and dealing with complaints as this gives the user ready access.

■ The local complaints register needs to record the date and nature of the complaint, who dealt with the problem, how it was resolved and by when. Service users can then see how well the system works.

■ It is more difficult to establish systems which cater for large-scale waste operations. For city-wide operations supporting a number of micro-enterprises, the local ward office may be the best place to register the complaints. Alternatively, a telephone system could be established for middle- and high- income areas.

Some examples

Resolving problems can be difficult. A common complaint by waste collectors concerns residents and shopkeepers who dump waste indiscriminately. This type of complaint should first be dealt with by discussion with the offender, but ultimately some sanction such as a fine should be available if the problem cannot be resolved informally.

Liaquat Town Welfare Society (Box 3) offered membership to the households living in the area and provided a waste collection service. The Society introduced and negotiated with four additional sweepers and residents were asked to pay a regular amount of Rs 20 per month per house to sweepers. Major problems were discussed in executive committee meetings. The Society initially registered more than 600 houses, ensured payments from residents to the sweepers and proper work from sweepers. Procedures to fire sweepers and punish defaulting residents were established. The complaint system is set up so that waste collectors and defaulters could both have equal access to it.

Box G11. Preparing the verbal/ written contracts

Problems

There needs to be an agreement between the service provider and the service user, which is mutually understood by all concerned. The agreement provides a safeguard to the rights of the various stakeholders.

Guidance

It is advisable to draw up some form of contract between the parties directly involved in a primary collection service.

- The actual form and detail required depends on the scale of the service. This could range from a verbal contract in the case of an activist organising a sweeper service to a comprehensive written contract for a service which encompasses many neighbourhoods.

- The contract must state the scope of work, define roles, responsibilities and penalties (if applicable) and must be known or signed by all the parties involved.

- In some cases the contract may serve as a guideline; other larger, more formal contracts must have legal status.

Some examples

Below are a few sample clauses paraphrased from a contract prepared under the FAUP in Faisalabad. Note that the FAUP, is responsible for implementing a wide range of local improvements is a 'special project organisation' which has an important role here; this is an exceptional case, as similar organisations are not widespread.

For Area Based Organisations (ABOs):

a) The organisation shall be responsible for the overall management of the primary collection programme. This includes hiring a sanitary worker, assuring regular and timely payments to the sanitary worker and monitoring performance of the sanitary worker. .

b) A sanitary worker may be a municipal sweeper or a self-employed private sweeper.

c) The ABO shall provide appropriate carts, tools and equipment to the sanitary worker in consultation with the FAUP staff.

Box G11. Preparing the verbal/ written contracts *(continued)*

d) In case of disputes the ABO and the sanitary worker may request a meeting of the advisory committee which will consist of a member from FAUP field office, area sanitary inspector and a member from the ABO.

e) In case of more than five complaints from the households in a month, the ABO shall call a meeting of the proposed advisory committee, which shall make the decision about the retrenchment of the sweeper.

Sanitary Worker's Responsibilities:

a) The sanitary worker will collect solid waste (household waste only excluding cow dung) from the individual houses at least six days a week.

b) The sanitary worker will clean the drains twice a week and remove solids from the drain.

c) The sanitary worker will not dispose of waste in the area or in the close vicinity. He will carry the waste to the nearest FMC transfer point.

d) The sanitary worker will not burn any waste in the area or away from the area.

Household Responsibilities:

a) Each household will pay a monthly fee of Rs. .... to the sanitary worker (or MPCO as mutually agreed) on or before the 5th of every month.

b) The sanitary worker as mutually agreed between the sanitary worker and the households shall additionally charge collection of extra quantities of waste (more than one bin per house). Similarly additional quantities of cow dung shall be removed for additional charges made to the sweeper.

c) If households are not satisfied with the performance of a sanitary worker they should report the matter to the MPCO as per attached form.

References

Ali M. et. al (1996), 'Municipal and the Informal Systems in Solid Waste Management'. In Educating for Real, Nabeel Hamdi and El Sherif A. (eds.). Intermediate Technology, Publications, UK.

Beall (1997), 'Households, Livelihoods and the Urban Environment: Social Development Perspectives on Solid Waste Management in Faisalabad, Pakistan'. Ph D Thesis, London School of Economics, University of London.

Streefland P. H. (1978), 'The Social Organisation of Night Soil Collection', in Sanitation in Developing Countries. Arnold Pacey (ed.). John Wiley and Sons, UK.

Annexe 1

Boxes

Box 1. Noor-ul-Amin Society, Millat Road, Faisalabad

Narrative

- In this case an area based organisation starts addressing primary collection issues. The residential estate was established in 1976, by the Cabinet Division Government of Pakistan for the rehabilitation of migrants from Bangladesh (Ex-East Pakistan) called Baharies, on the state land. Since no facilities were provided by the government at the time of the establishment of the colony, people started getting organised in order to get basic services. At this early stage, a loosely organised group of people made efforts to procure electricity, drainage and street paving.

- Meanwhile, when the Government imposed instalment fees on the previously free houses, people seriously thought of an association through which they could lobby for their rights. Four years after the establishment of the colony, the residents formed an organisation named Millat Welfare Society in 1980.

- The Society is registered with the Social Welfare Department under the Voluntary Organisation Registration and Control Act.

- For the primary collection of solid waste, the Society has acquired additional staff from FMC to monitor their work and have direct liaison with FMC head office.

- There is no prescribed method of payment. Sweepers get some money as tips on special days and occasions.

Commentary

- People are getting services and infrastructure through a number of mechanisms.
- Solid waste comes lower in the hierarchy of need for services and infrastructure.

- Common problem acted as a trigger to the formation of the Society

- Registration is important to establish credibility with other residents and with government departments in order to act as a pressure group.

- The established credibility of registration is now working.
- There is a dependency on the municipal sector.
- Possibly negative impacts on sweepers' existing entrepreneurship.

- The approach adopted is not favourable to the development of sustainable micro-enterprises, as the payments are not regular.

Box 2. Muslim Town Welfare Society, Muslim Town, Faisalabad

Narrative	Commentary
■ Muslim Town was developed as a residential area by a private developer on agricultural land. At the time when the land was sold to the people, the only services in the area were electricity, constructed roads and sewerage. People who bought land were fully aware of this fact. Since there was little infrastructure available in the area, residents gave this issue a high priority.	■ Solid waste comes lower in the hierarchy of need for services and infrastructure.
■ At that time some activists in the area floated an idea for the formation of a community-based organisation so that they could facilitate the development of the area. The idea was encouraged and appreciated by the majority of people. In this way the Society was established on 24th May, 1988 and got registration with the Social Welfare Department. The society prepared its constitution which binds all the members to obey any decisions taken by their repre-sentative.	■ Absence of a number of services and infrastructure triggers the idea of forming an organization.
■ On its formation, the welfare society made private arrangements for a sweeper to clean the streets.	■ Perhaps a temporary arrangement in the absence of a municipal service.
■ Until May 1994 Muslim Town fell outside the municipal boundaries and therefore did not have access to a municipal waste collection service.	■ Residents felt that inclusion in the municipal area would also resolve the waste collection problem.
■ Since May 1994 Muslim Town has had a regular municipal service, but households still pay a regular amount of Rs. 20 to 50 to the sweepers.	■ The sweepers succeeded in negotiating and collecting fees from residents, thereby sustaining the system. ■ The inclusion of Muslim Town within the municipal limits did not change the process through which residents receive a primary collection service and make payments.

Box 3. Liaquat Town Welfare Society, Liaquat Town, Faisalabad

Narrative

- A private developer developed Liaquat town area in 1980. He got final approval from FDA according to their byelaws. At the time when plots were sold to people there was electricity, a paved road, a waste collection service provided by private sweepers and spaces for a dispensary, primary school, high school and mosque.

- The area of the colony is about 66 acres. There are 625 demarcated plots of different sizes ranging from 5-20 marlas in four blocks. There were very few facilities available at that time which made people think of forming their own organisation. The idea was generated and floated to residents by an eminent person, Haji Abdul Hameed. Some people who agreed to the formation of the society encouraged the idea.

- People were openly offered membership. Each household living in the area was eligible for membership. All the members selected ten executives who were allocated different responsibilities and started work in the area .

- Since there were a number of issues to be tackled by the Society they decided to prioritise these issues. As a result, Sui gas (fuel for cooking) became their top priority. When the Society contacted the gas department, they demanded that the Society should be registered. In this way, the Society became registered with the Social Welfare Department in 1990 under the Voluntary Organisations Registration and Control Act. The Society also drafted its constitution, which is respected by the selected representatives as well as general members.

- Introduction and negotiation with four additional sweepers to the area was done. Residents were asked to pay a regular amount of Rs 20 per month per house to sweepers. The Society initially involved more than 600 houses, ensuring payments from residents to the sweepers and ensuring proper work from sweepers. Prescribed methods to dismiss sweepers and punish defaulting residents were established.

Commentary

- A private developer gives priority to a waste collection system in order to enhance the status of the area and therefore the value of the properties.

- To retain the system, there is a need for area-based organisations.

- Common issues of acquiring services and infrastructure act as a trigger to the formation of the society.

- Registration is important to establish credibility with other residents and utilities departments in order to act as a pressure group.

- Not only is the right type of organisation available in terms of establishment, trust, credibility and structure but their approach supports the existing entrepreneurship of sweepers.

Box 4. M. A. Jinnah Development Society, Shadab Colony, Faisalabad

Narrative	Commentary
■ Some youngsters from around the area shared the idea for the formation of the organisation ten years ago. They formed a group and started to do charity works such as blood donations and a free dispensary.	■ Trigger to the formation of the Society is not infrastructure and services but regular charity work concerning health.
■ In February 1996, Faisalabad Area Upgrading Project (FAUP) approached this area for the formation of a community-based organisation. The FAUP team contacted two activists of the existing organisation who had played an active role in its formation. They helped in arranging the meetings and in conveying FAUP's strategy to each household of their neighbourhood.	■ Strengthening of the Society takes place because of problems related to infrastructure and services. Role of the external agency is seen as important.
■ Motivation for the formation of Multi Purpose Community Organisations (MPCO) came mainly from FAUP. Guidelines are given by FAUP on how to make these most effective by popular participation. People in this locality have a number of shared interests they want to take up such as the main road construction, water supply, development of the parks and a solid waste management system.	■ There is always scope available for an external support agency like FAUP to play a positive role.
■ Introductions and negotiations with one private and one municipal sweeper were made for a primary waste collection service. The Society has asked residents to pay a regular amount and the programme involves more than 100 houses.	■ Not only is the right type of organisation available but the approach supports the existing entrepreneurship of sweepers.
■ A loan was provided to the sweeper to buy a donkey cart. Appropriate designs were prepared and manufactured by FAUP. In addition, cleanliness campaigns were organised. Social pressure was exerted on defaulters.	■ Entrepreneurial risk is reduced by providing loans, increasing awareness and demand, and by acting against defaulters.
■ Sweepers charge Rs 20 per month per house for the primary collection service. Sweepers pay 25% to M. A. Jinnah for the community works.	

Box 5. Sulemaina Welfare Society, Fat-he-Abad, Faisalabad

Narrative	Commentary
■ Fat-he-Abad is an old settlement, established before the independence of Pakistan (1947). It was an illegal settlement on state land and was recognised and developed by FDA in 1985.	
■ The majority of the residents belong to the lower middle or low-income group. The area is served by a sewerage system, brick paving in the streets, electricity, gas, street lights, water supply etc.	■ Primary collection initiatives are not restricted to middle and high-income areas.
■ A few older residents of the area floated the idea for the formation of a society, as they were unhappy that young girls had to go outside the area in order to get vocational training such as simple stitching and sewing training. They came to know that the Social Welfare Department provides support in establishing vocational centres provided that they are registered with the Department.	■ Formation of the organisation is triggered because of a specific need other than infrastructure and services.
■ The group made an announcement over the loud speaker for a meeting regarding the registration and introduction of the organisation.	
■ The society has acquired additional sweepers from FMC and arranged the transfer of existing sweepers, who were not covering the area. Payment of Rs 2 per week per house to sweepers was also arranged.	■ Right type of organisation is available. Liaison with municipal corporation and payment to sweepers are important elements of micro-enterprise development. ■ Payments to sweepers may be very small in low-income areas.

Box 6. Ayub Welfare Society, Ayub Colony, Faisalabad

Narrative

- Ayub colony was established in 1976 by a private developer on private land. At the time of development, the developer provided very basic infrastructure and services. This colony has 12 streets and the usual plot size is 5 marla. Most of the people are engaged with their personal business such as power-looms and some run their own shops. There are a few who are engaged with the loading and unloading of textiles. Although there are different caste groups the community feel united by their collective efforts and have obtained sewers, electricity and gas from the departments concerned.

- The idea of the formation of the Society is very recent, dating from a time when some land grabbers tried to occupy the state land, about one acre, adjacent to Ayub Colony. They tried their best to keep the illegal occupier away and informed different government departments, but the person was quite influential. He somehow, managed to get a court statement in his favour, but the community did not give up and obtained a status quo order. This incident gave the people a chance to pool their resources and to form an association to deal with this issue.

- They were told by one of their friends that they should have their collective association recognised by the department as a Society. Then the eminent members of the Society called a meeting to discuss the idea of the formation of the Society and to offer membership to like-minded people. About 60 people became members. The Society became registered with the Social Welfare Department in 1993.

- For primary waste collection, the Society regularly monitors the sweepers and is interested in expanding the work to other areas. Some houses pay the sweepers Rs 3 per house per week.

Commentary

- Infrastructure and services were acquired through collective efforts but without any structured organisation.

- Common problems acted as a trigger to the formation of the Society.

- Registration is important to establish credibility with other residents and government departments in order to act as a pressure group.

- The right type of organisation is available but needs assistance in developing the primary collection programme.

Box 7. Green Peace Welfare, Firdous Colony, Faisalabad

Narrative

- Firdous Colony was developed by a private developer in the early 1960s. Very basic infrastructure and services were available at the time of occupation. The majority of the residents are migrants from other areas and belong to different caste groups. After people had constructed their houses, the government departments began the development works, such as sewers and electricity provision. The main bazaar road was metalled in 1973.

- There were no open spaces left for community services and later the land reserved for the school was also sold. The community resisted and lobbied for the transfer of land to Faisalabad Municipal Corporation (FMC). The FMC initially started the school in a rented house and because of continuous demand from the community, the residents succeeded in getting funds for the school in 1980. Now they have regular girls' and boys' schools in their area.

- In 1990 a society called Young Welfare Society was formed in the area but it could not be sustained due to embezzlement of their funds. Then four young persons from the area inspired by an international organisation called Greenpeace decided to form a society which they decided to name Green Peace.

- At the time when the Society was formed, they called an area level meeting, inviting all the caste groups to become members, as the Society will not identify itself on the basis of caste, religion and politics. The society is not registered with any department, yet they have their management structure.

- The Society was able to get an additional seven sweepers for the area from FMC. They asked residents to regularly pay Rs 3 per house per week to sweepers. They obtained one marla of land from Ayub Research Institute in return for waste (as fertiliser) for the Institute.

Commentary

- Formation of the organisation is triggered by the specific need for a school rather than conventional infrastructure such as sewerage and drainage.

- New organisations replace the existing ones based on caste and heredity.

- Organised group could get additional staff from municipal corporation.
- Payments to sweepers are on the low side and perhaps paid as tips rather than collection charges.
- In order to retain the sweepers the community organisation must guarantee regular payments in a more systematic way.

Box 8. New Public Welfare Society, Saifabad, Faisalabad

Narrative	Commentary
■ A private developer started selling plots in 1976. The land was subdivided into 19 streets comprising different categories of plots. Two school sites (about 22 kanals land in total) and one plot for a mosque were also provided. The proprietor did not provide any services in the area. Since the streets were quite wide and the ground water was drinkable, the people were willing to buy the land even in the absence of any infrastructure.	
■ The sweeping and waste collection services from the FMC are negligible in this area.	■ Peripheral areas within municipal limits receive lesser services.
■ Since there were no facilities available in the area and the people living in the colony were facing many difficulties, the people decided to form a welfare society to tackle their problems. This was the Public Welfare Society - Saifabad, formed in 1989.	■ Un-availability of services and infrastructure was a trigger to the formation of the Society.
■ In the beginning there were 30 members and every member was contributing Rs 10 per month. The Society took the issue of provision of electricity in the colony as their first priority. With the efforts of the Society, the colony got the electricity. After some time, the members showed their reluctance to pay the membership fees and the Society was meeting regularly without any contributions. In 1991, the area obtained the facility of Natural Gas. The Society remained functional for different issues related to the area. In 1996, the Society succeeded in obtaining a main sewer line costing Rs:5 lacs paid for out of the MPA fund.	■ Collective action is important to acquire services and infrastructure. ■ Regular payments without the provision of a service are difficult to sustain. ■ Capacity to acquire funds from a variety of sources.
■ After the success of getting sanctioned funds for the main sewer line, the people became more confident and started organising themselves at the lane	■ Residents recognise the importance of collective efforts and are ready to contribute their share.

Box 8. New Public Welfare Society, Saifabad, Faisalabad *(continued)*

Narrative	Commentary
level for the laying of lane sewers. To date, the residents have laid the lane sewers in 70 % of the streets and spent about Rs 12 lacs of their own. Since the residents laid these lines without any technical guidance, some of the lines have subsequently become blocked and other technical problems have arisen.	■ There is scope for an external agency to support some of these actions.
■ Until 1996, the Society worked in the capacity of an un-registered Society. In the year 1996 they registered their Society in the name of New Public Welfare Society. At the time of registration, the Society elected the new office bearer.	■ Registration is important to establish credibility with other residents and government departments in order to act as a pressure group.
■ Introductions and negotiations with one private sweeper were carried out and the Society asked residents to pay Rs 10 per month per house to the sweeper.	■ After consolidation of the organisation, the right approach is adopted to hire and pay the sweeper for primary waste collection.

Box 9. Suzuki System, Karachi, Pakistan

Narrative	Commentary
■ The waste collection programme using Suzukis (a type of small truck common in the city) was initiated in 1988 by a local activist. In 1988 he was a member of *'Mushawarat Council'* (advisory council), an alternative representation from the area which replaced elected local councillors. However, later that activist was elected as a councillor from the same area.	■ Elected representatives and local politicians also initiate non-conventional programmes. ■ Local politicians could be an important link between the residents and the municipal corporation.
■ According to the activist, there was a great demand by the residents at that time for a cleaner neighbourhood environment He had been receiving complaints about scattered waste and un-collected waste piles in the area.	■ The area is well served with infrastructure and services and so the need for a proper waste collection service arises.

Box 9. Suzuki System, Karachi, Pakistan *(continued)*

Narrative	Commentary
■ People were also requesting the shifting of transfer points from their vicinity, which could only be removed if all the waste was brought to a single point using vehicles.	■ The need for a house to house collection system arose to get rid of transfer points and scattered waste piles in the neighbourhood. This is the initial, primary incentive to start a house to house collection system.
■ As a first step, the programme organiser distributed letters to all the 1,000 houses in the area, informing them about the proposed programme and the monthly fee that they would have to pay. In response, he received a 'go ahead' reply from about 950 families out of the 1000 letters issued (as reported by the programme organiser).	■ The proposed programme and fees are announced. ■ No motivation and awareness raising campaign was done but residents participated in the programme.
■ Two used Suzuki vans were purchased, one for Rs 20,000 and other for Rs 25,000, and the bodywork adapted for use as waste collection vehicles. A collection service was started sometime in 1988.	■ The capital expenditures were kept low and provided from personal resources.
■ The Suzuki system was not used by all the residents in the beginning and the system received waste from only 650 houses instead of the 950 families who agreed in the first instance. Gradually, almost all the houses in the area joined the service.	■ Although 950 agreed to join, only 650 actually joined the programme, the remainder continued with the existing sweepers' system.
■ Some houses were also reluctant to pay a monthly fee for the waste collection service, which was fixed at Rs 15 per month at that time which was increased to Rs 25 in 1994. The programme organiser instructed the collection crew to collect waste from all the houses, whether they were paying monthly charges or not.	■ Demonstrating the impact of waste collection service was also important.
■ When the programme started, the Suzukis used to dispose of the collected waste at the official disposal area in the North of Karachi, which is about 10 km away from the project area.	■ Transfer of waste from primary collection stage to secondary transportation is an important interface with the municipality.

Box 9. Suzuki System, Karachi, Pakistan *(continued)*

Narrative	Commentary
However, after a few months they found it expensive to dispose of waste at the disposal site. There were also problems from traffic police on the major roads. The programme organiser therefore constructed a walled enclosure using his councillor's funds, in a playground within the programme area.	■ A playground was misused to store the waste.
■ The programme soon developed and gained popularity among residents. In this way waste from 1,000 houses was brought to a single transfer point. Residents got a reliable service for which they were willing to pay.	■ Reliable service, cleaner streets and removal of waste transfer points played a key role in popularity of the service.
■ The political rise and fall of the programme organiser took place during the period 1988 to 1994 which affected the programme. However, in spite of all the problems, the programme operated until 1994.	■ Political context is important and there is always a need to under-stand the power structure.
■ Although the programme stopped its operation in 1994, citizens of Karachi got the idea as to how such systems could be operated. In 1998, several programmes were operating in the city on similar principles.	■ The programme was stopped because of the political rise and fall of the activists. ■ Although little documentation is available, the programme acted as a demonstration.

Box 10. Gram Shampad Unnayan Kendra, Green Road Area, Dhaka

Narrative	Commentary
■ Gram Shampad Unnayan Kendra is a self-financing NGO whose head office is in Green Road, a middle-income area. They are involved in activities such as income generation, health, family planning, mass education and forestry.	
■ Solid waste management in the area was very poor before 1994. DCC did not provide bins in the area. The residents did not want to have bins near to their houses. It was also observed that where bins were provided, they were not cleaned regularly by the DCC cleaner.	■ The NGO is well aware of the problems in the area.
■ Considering the poor conditions of waste, in 1994 the executive committee of the NGO decided to take some initiative on solid waste management. At first the executive committee was not certain about the number of households to be included in the solid waste management programme. Finally, they decided to include 250 households under their programme.	■ Decision to initiate a programme comes from the executive committee of the NGO in response to the perceived needs of the local community. ■ Number of houses to be included has no logical basis. Ideally, it must be based on demand.
■ Before fixing the service charge per household, contact was made with the local leaders and with the ward commissioner (elected representative). Everybody expressed their full support for the programme.	■ The programme was designed first and then community members were contacted.
■ Gram Shampad Unnayan Kendra bought one rickshaw van and other equipment such as spades, plastic baskets, shovels and rakes. At first, the rickshaw van wheel spokes were thin, but these were later replaced with strong spokes. The rickshaw van is now strong and it cost Tk. 1200. A box was also built on the van.	■ The NGO acts as a service providing organisation. ■ Technology continued to be modified on the basis of experienced gained.
■ The community through leaflet distribution has been informed of	■ Not much done on community awareness campaign.

Box 10. Gram Shampad Unnayan Kendra, Green Road Area, Dhaka
(continued)

Narrative	Commentary
the waste collection time and where dwellers should bring their household waste.	
■ A DCC daily wage sweeper was hired. The waste collection time was scheduled between 10:00 a.m. and 4:00 p.m. Sweeper would get Tk 1000 per month from the project. It was decided that the sweeper would go to every household and ring the bell. The dwellers would come down into the street and hand over the polythene bags with waste. The sweepers would take the bags and put them into the van. When the van was full, the sweeper would take the waste van to the metal container provided by DCC. The distance from the waste collection area to Green Road is about 200 yards.	■ A nearby transfer point is available, which may not be the case for all the areas.
■ A service charge (of Tk. 5) was levied per month for each household.	
■ Two more people, an adult and a waste picker were hired to collect the waste. Accordingly, for improved services the sweepers would collect household waste directly from the houses and for these the service charge would be Tk. 5 to Tk. 20.	■ Waste pickers hired to reduce the cost. ■ Service charges increased.
■ Many dwellers failed to bring their household waste bags to the waste collection van in time. Thus many houses were missed in the collection of waste.	■ There are problems in the start-up of the programme.
■ One sweeper now gets Tk. 2500 another one gets Tk. 1000 and the waste picker gets Tk. 300 per month. Sometimes the sweepers get tips during festivals or other special occasions. All three workers are male. They not only collect household waste but also sweep the roads around the catchment area twice a day. About 10 to 15 percent of dwellers do	■ Different salaries for the same work. ■ Non payment of service charges may cause problems with sustainability.

Box 10. Gram Shampad Unnayan Kendra, Green Road Area, Dhaka
(continued)

Narrative	Commentary
not pay their service charges regularly. So, there is a shortfall of Tk. 300- 400 every month.	
■ Gram Shampad Unnayan Kendra has planned to extend their solid waste collection activities to other areas. The areas are Pallabi and Kathal Bagan (middle class income group area).	■ It is not clear what lessons are learned and what is the basis of expansion.
■ They also plan to expand their activities on solid waste management to two private slums in other areas without any service charges. In future the Gram Shampad Unnayan Kendra will provide two plastic bags to every household for the separation of organic and non-organic waste.	■ It is difficult to sustain the system without service charges.

Box 11. Kashmirtola Area, Dhaka

Narrative	Commentary
■ The Kashmirtola area is located in the old Dhaka City where roads are narrow. The area is densely populated with middle and low income groups.	■ It is always difficult to organize a waste collection system in such areas.
■ The solid waste collection programme was started in mid 1995. It was claimed as a self initiated solid waste management activity, although the society members had received encouragement by the Environmental Health Programme of ICDDR,B. The neighborhood committee was formed with the help of ICDDR,B but without political influences, and included one member from every family. Committee members received training on water, sanitation and health issues from ICDDR,B.	■ An international NGO convince the local community group to initiate the change.

Box 11. Kashmirtola Area, Dhaka (continued)

Narrative	Commentary
■ The neighborhood committee decided to work on solid waste management in the Kashmirtola area. The committee sought the opinion of the community, and received their approval.	■ The community is involved at the planning stage.
■ The committee members requested the ward commissioner (elected representative of local bodies) to remove all the dustbins from the area, as nobody liked dustbins near their houses. Accordingly, all the dustbins were removed.	■ The ward commissioner assists the community in the removal of dustbins.
■ It was decided that every dweller would keep his/her household waste in polythene bags and a DCC sweeper would come and collect the household waste and take it to the transfer point with a hand trolley. A bell was bought by the committee and handed over to the DCC sweeper. The DCC sweeper would ring the bell then the dweller would come into the lane and the waste bags would be handed over to the sweeper. As the sweepers are from DCC, the dwellers do not have to pay any money for the service. Sweepers get some tips if they collect waste from multi-storied buildings or from factories.	■ There is a dependency on the DCC system without any payments to sweepers. ■ Such systems are difficult to sustain.
■ Two sweepers were engaged for this work. The neighborhood committee members supervise the work of the sweepers. If the sweepers are not attending the area regularly, then households could complain to the committee.	■ A system of complaints also formed.
■ Recently, they formed a cooperative society with a membership of 400. Each member deposited Tk. 100 per month to the society. The name of the society is "Naboprodit" which means new light. Their future plan is to eradicate mosquitoes.	■ A collective action around primary collection paved the way for a co-operative society. ■ The formation of the co-operative society could sustain the programme and continuous payments to sweepers.

Box 12. Rana Jagoroni Club, Jigatoal area, Dhaka

Narrative

- The Jigatoal area is a middle class income group area with a number of multi-storied buildings and wide road provisions. The Rana Jagoroni club was established in 1965 by a business man in handicraft and other trades; a social organizer with political affiliations. The main activities of the club are to organize games, cultural activities and social works. They observed all the national days and initiated blood donation programmes with the perceived objectives of community welfare.

- In 1995, the executive committee of the club initiated a street sweeping project to improve the local environmental situation.

- The community needs were assessed by means of a survey. A club member was authorized to hire a sweeper. Two sweepers who live at Gonoktuly sweeper colony, one male and one female, were appointed. Each sweeper received Tk. 3000 as their monthly salary and in addition to that received Tk. 500 as a bonus for the Eid festival.

- A hand trolley, a bell and a register were given to the sweepers by the club. The residents were informed about the waste collection schedule; they would place their household waste near their respective gates when the sweepers ring the bell. The sweepers would not collect the waste directly from the houses but they would collect it from the gate and take it to the dustbin (metal container). For this each household paid Tk. 20 every month as a service charge.

- Four hundred households were included in this programme. The sweepers collected the monthly service charge from each household within the first week of

Commentary

- Motivation to form a community based organization is not based on the provision of infrastructure and services.

- The decision to start the programme is from the executive committee.

- Collection fee is fixed from the inception of the programme.

- Sweepers productivity reduces while collecting money.

Box 12. Rana Jagoroni Club, Jigatoal area, Dhaka *(continued)*

Narrative	**Commentary**
every month. The residents sign the register to indicate that they have paid. The sweepers deposited the money collected with the club authority.	
■ If any new resident comes to the area then club members make contact and include them in the solid waste management programme. Sometimes the club activists pay visits to the members' houses to find out about the problems regarding solid waste. A regular annual meeting also takes place in the club where solid waste management reports are discussed.	■ A monitoring system is established.
■ In future they plan to expand their solid waste management activities to other areas of electoral ward 48. To that end, they have already circulated leaflets to every household. They have also planned to provide two polythene bags to each household to store organic and non-organic kitchen waste.	■ Continuous expansion and improvement of the programme is on the agenda.

Box 13. Kamal Chowdhry, Ward 36, Dhaka

Narrative	**Commentary**
■ A recently elected Ward Commissioner was informed that solid waste, broken roads and terrorism were the major problems in the area. The roads were narrow, two vehicles could not pass side by side and there were many DCC provided dustbins. Waste was dumped in these dustbins throughout the day and these were kept dirty, smelly and attracted flies and insects.	■ The communal dust bins provided by DCC were perceived as a nuisance in the area.
■ A proposal was made to the Honorable Mayor of Dhaka City to	■ City level political commitment was sought.

72

Box 13. Kamal Chowdhry, Ward 36, Dhaka *(continued)*

Narrative	Commentary
demolish all the dustbins, clean the roads and organise house to house collections by van in order to solve the problem. The mayor suggested that two pilot projects should be started.	
■ Later it was realized that such a project would require about 12 vans at a cost of 7000 - 8000 Taka. Local businessmen were approached for donations and a positive response was received.	■ Private funding opportunities were explored. ■ A comparatively large scale programme was started.
■ In 1995, 12 vans were purchased, an announcement was made and leaflets were distributed among local people informing them about the new system. It was planned that these vans would go every-where and ring a bell in front of every house. People were expected to hand over their waste to the vans every afternoon.	
■ These vans collected waste from households and dumped it at newly installed containers set by the side of main roads. Gradually, residents have joined the system.	
■ The service was free while the costs were borne by DCC and private funding. However, people sometimes give 5 to 10 Taka tips to the van drivers.	■ Residents have not been asked to pay collection fees so there is no mechanism for cost recovery. This may result in a dependency on DCC.
■ Out of all DCC sweepers in the area, 12 work on vans and the rest perform street sweeping. The vans collect waste from 5 p.m. to 8 p.m. The van drivers know every house and sometime knock at the doors of the houses if they do not give waste.	■ Waste is collected in the evenings.
■ The ward commissioner sponsors some of the vans and pays for repairs and maintenance from his funds. The name of the donor of the van is also painted on it. The van drivers receive a salary from DCC and tips from some families.	■ Donors are given recognition.

Box 13. Kamal Chowdhry, Ward 36, Dhaka (continued)

Narrative	Commentary
Two of the vans were stolen after the inception of the programme.	
■ Now, the honorable Mayor is considering replicating the same system in Dhaka city and called a meeting to discuss it. He has agreed to form waste disposal committees at zonal, ward and Mohollah levels. There will be volunteers to promote and supervise it.	■ Political will at the city level is fully supportive. Links with ward commissioners and councillors are important.
■ The ward commissioner is a political figure who is not in favour of fee collection, as he may be blamed for being corrupt. He is happy to maintain a free of charge service as long as he can manage it.	■ Politicians are reluctant to fix the collection charge.
■ He thinks that the system could be used in old Dhaka City, where there are narrow roads and overcrowded streets. These vans can run through narrow roads. The system is considered as 90% successful.	

Box 14. Mahbub Ahsan, Kolabghan Area, Dhaka

Narrative	Commentary
■ The situation regarding management of solid waste was extremely poor before 1987, when the programme started. The organiser (Mahbub Ahsan) initially considered starting something with a single lane.	■ Pilot scale activities must ideally start with the smallest possible unit.
■ The City Corporation provided bins but locating space to place the bins was a major problem. Nobody wanted a dustbin near their house and they were continually moved from one place to another.	■ Communal bins again appeared as a major nuisance.

Box 14. Mahbub Ahsan, Kolabghan Area, Dhaka *(continued)*

Narrative	Commentary
■ Initially, a once-a-week collection system was considered but the waste soon begins to smell because of the heat. Then it was thought to buy a collection van for waste collection from the whole area and removal to a far away place. Finally the programme started with 250 houses and one cycle rickshaw was purchased.	■ The number of houses was fixed rather randomly, but was possibly based on the existence of the social network.
■ There are also a number of flats in the area and the residents liked to have a collection service from their doors. They pay an additional amount of money (tips) to sweepers so that they will go upstairs and collect waste.	■ The physical layout and housing type affects the programme operation.
■ The programme has gradually expanded and now the programme collects waste from 700 houses, which are on the register. A number of shops do not pay, but are usually asked to hand over waste, otherwise they will throw garbage into the street. Now two rickshaw vehicles operate, each with a team of three sweepers, making about 3 to 3.5 trips every day. Each trip carries waste from 100 to 120 houses.	■ Gradual expansion of the programme is a sign of success and sustainability. ■ The programme organiser collects the money and keeps the profits.
■ Sweepers working on the programme are either municipal employees or their relatives. The main advantage of employing municipal sweepers is that they know the area as they already collect waste from a number of houses. There is also a stand-by sweeper and a salaried person to collect money from the houses.	■ Employing municipal sweepers working in the area avoids undue complications in the form of competition. ■ Money collection has been considered as a separate task and is not delegated to the sweeper.
■ There is daily collection. The rickshaws are modified to have steel wheels and a metallic box (Size 6ft X 3 ft X 3.5 ft) at the back. Sweepers just pull and push the rickshaw.	■ Technology is modified gradually.
■ There are many problems in money collection, over 10% of residents	■ There are problems collecting dues from some of the residents.

Box 14. Mahbub Ahsan, Kolabghan Area, Dhaka (continued)

Narrative	Commentary
and tenants continually ask the money collector return later.	
■ A number of visitors came to visit their programme. The German cultural centre in Dhaka made a video of their programme and another video was made by CIDA, which has been shown on television. It appears on the television twice a week. CIDA prepared the video and the Ministry of Information sponsored it for television.	■ The programme has acquired city wide recognition.
■ Now the programme has replaced the old rickshaws with new ones. These cost Tk 18,000 each. They have used a 16 gauge metallic galvanised iron sheet, but it is frequently damaged while waste is being un-loaded with a scraper.	■ Savings have been kept carefully and used for repair, maintenance and replacement of vehicles.
■ Painting also needs to be done frequently.	
■ Vehicles are smelly and it is difficult to park them inside the house. The programme is popular and Mahbub gets a lot of requests on a lane basis every day. Sweepers separate paper, plastics, bottles etc.from the waste for resale.	
■ Secondary collection from containers has been a problem, Mahbub has the authority to go to the Chief Engineer's office directly (other people in low income areas may not do this). The main road where the container is placed is a 'VIP' road, so the city corporation does not like to keep a container on that road. Consequently the city corporation asked them to take waste to a concrete enclosure in another place.	■ There are problems with secondary collection. ■ Links with ward commissioner and DCC are not established and depend upon a number of personal relationships.
■ The Ward Commissioner did not view the programme positively. On one occasion the Ward Commissioner stopped the	■ Apparently, there is competition between the Ward Commissioner and the activist.

Box 14. Mahbub Ahsan, Kolabghan Area, Dhaka *(continued)*

Narrative	Commentary
rickshaw and said that since he did not have a trade licence, he could not collect waste. Mahbub arranged the trade licence the next day. Fortunately, the Chief Engineer of City Corporation is in the same area and has assisted Mahbub in resolving such conflicts.	
■ Since 1987 the collection fee charged was Tk 10 per month, but in April 1996 it was increased to Tk 15 per month. Mahbub pays the sweepers a salary of Tk 1200 per month. The conservancy inspectors (supervisors) in the area are happy, since they claim that now their area is cleaned by Mahbub's programme.	
■ Now, Action Aid, an NGO working in the Mohammad Pur Area would like to start a similar programme. Other people in adjacent areas are also operating similar programmes. Some areas are difficult, since there are a number of shops and other commercial activities. A number of waste pickers were interested in working with the system, but it is difficult, since sweepers do not want to share their income.	■ An international NGO learns the principles of the programme from a small scale contractor. (See box 15) ■ Competition among different groups of workers is possible.
■ Since all the sweepers are male, they have problems in entering houses. A number of residents ask them to collect construction debris and garden waste, but it is often difficult to dispose of such wastes.	
■ Mahbub emphasises that the size of the project must be small (for example not more than 1000 houses). If it is a large scale contract, it will become another municipal corporation according to Mahbub. He is willing to train and advise other people in setting up small scale waste collection programmes.	

Box 15. Action Aid's programme in Shyamoli, Dhaka

Narrative	Commentary
■ The dustbins in the neighbourhood of the NGOs office were overflowing with refuse. This was creating an unhealthy environment for the residents, and was an unwelcome sight to guests visiting the NGOs office. Therefore, a plan was drawn up to clean up the area and provide a basic service. It was envisaged that the programme would be handed over to local residents once it was functioning satisfactorily.	■ The programme was initiated by an international NGO working in the area. ■ The level of cleanliness was judged by the NGO. ■ The vision of handing over the programme to the community is important, once it is demonstrated successfully at the pilot stage.
■ There are 552 middle income families in the the programme area (162 house owners and 390 tenant families). In addition, there are 411 families in slums.	■ Detailed information from surveys is available.
■ The programme commenced operation in March 1997. All of the households give their waste to the appointed collector. However, only the house owners pay. That is, the tenants of middle-income households and the slum dwellers do not pay for the service. There are 162 house owners who pay Taka 10-20 per month. Owners of flats with many tenant families pay more. This charge has been mutually agreed upon.	■ There is an indication of cross-subsidy from high and middle income to low income groups. ■ The poor obtain the service free of charge.
■ The programme employs three people. There is one supervisor whose salary is Taka 100 per day. There are two sweepers who are paid Taka 750 per month. All are male. Both the sweepers are DCC workers. They have been working on the programme from the beginning.	
■ A supervisor goes from door to door to collect the charges. Initially, he faced some problems from an influential resident who was opposed to the programme.	■ Money collection is considered as a separate task.
■ Mr. Mahbub Ahsan of Kolabagan (see Box 14) designed the vans. His help was sought because he	■ There is evidence of learning from other projects.

Box 15. Action Aid's programme in Shyamoli, Dhaka *(continued)*

Narrative	Commentary
had experimented with different types of vans in the course of his programme. The vans cost approximately Taka 17,000 each.	
■ There are no problems with the placement of secondary collection containers and the waste is regularly collected from these containers. So DCC workers are co-operating in this effort.	■ Is this because of the involvement of Action Aid ?
■ The Ward Commissioner was very co-operative in the beginning and also promised to assign sweepers. Action Aid was only able to provide vans. He also expressed willingness to request local youths to provide support to the programme. However, he later became antagonistic. He started his own similar programme in other areas. It is possible that he thought all the credit was being given to Action Aid and he was being deprived.	■ Relationship with the ward commissioner has not worked well and he became a competitor to the programme.
■ The project is perceived as sustainable. The transfer of this operation to local residents is being considered. It is believed that an NGO should not continue to provide such service forever. This work has to be done by the community. It is possible that the supervisor may continue this work. However, whether he will be able to withstand opposition from influential quarters is something to be observed. Furthermore, being an international NGO there is some influence and people do not easily harass the NGO. This may not be the case with local operators.	■ Transferring of the project may be an interesting phase. ■ NGO accepts that it could influence official agencies, while small enterprises may not be able to. ■ How could such influence be transferred to the community in order to sustain the project?

Box 16. Perveen's programme in Charaon Nagar, Dhaka

Narrative

- Perveen is a housewife and also a social organiser with some political affiliations in the area of Charaon Nagar. She is the only lady who came forward to organise the community around a solid waste collection programme, when ICDDR,B contacted the residents for health and hygiene programmes.

- This area has been inhabited for more than 30 years. Streets are paved and have an average width of only 8 ft. The area is unplanned but not very overcrowded.

- In her efforts to organise a system, she made contacts with the Ward Commissioner, hired a sweeper and started this work. The area is much cleaner and improved now, as before the system was in place, residents used to throw waste on the streets.

- Before the house to house collection system initiated by Perveen, there was no sweeper attending the area. Since there are a number of tanneries in the vicinity, the overall environment was also poor. ICDDR organised residents into neighbourhood committees. They also invited Ward Commissioners to their meetings and discussed the problem of solid waste. The Ward Commissioner tried to send sweepers and promised that if sweepers would not attend the area he would take some action. Even then, sweepers did not attend the area regularly.

- Finally, she contacted a sweeper and promised to pay him Tk 10 per month per house (minimum) from 100 houses. Now all the houses pay money directly to the sweeper. Perveen could not collect money because of a number of other responsibilities. All the households

Commentary

- Political affiliation may act as an incentive, besides other motivational factors.

- The ICDDR, B, an NGO, initiated an awareness raising campaign in the area.

- When the other basic services are available, solid waste collection becomes a higher priority.

- Contact with the Ward Commissioner may always be the starting point.

- Impact on the local environment is positive.

- Sweepers do not attend the low income areas because of low income opportunities.

- The Ward Commissioner could not guarantee a sustainable system.

- Regular payments play a key role in getting primary collection service in the existing system.

Box 16. Perveen's programme in Charaon Nagar, Dhaka *(continued)*

Narrative	Commentary
were asked to pay their contribution to sweepers in the first week of every month. If households do not pay, the sweeper complains to Perveen and she tries to sort the problem out.	
■ They also asked sweepers to take the waste away from the area, however, there was no secondary collection point in the area. No other support to the sweeper was provided through this programme. The sweeper comes in the evening. Cleaning of the street is a municipal duty and the sweeper does not charge any money for this service. He does not perform this service daily, but does it quite regularly.	■ Support to the sweeper could have been useful.
■ As a few families did not pay in the beginning, Perveen had meetings with them and explained about the adverse health effects of poor waste management. She also told people that in order to keeps the area cleaner, they must give their waste to the sweeper, even if they do not pay money. Eventually, most of the 100 families started to pay money and give waste to sweepers.	■ Trust and participation in the programme builds gradually.
■ Those who can afford it pay excess money to the sweeper. It does not depend upon the quantity of waste collected nor on any other factor. The female sweeper on the programme is the employee of the municipal corporation and her son helps her in sweeping roads. Her son also collects waste from 100 houses. There are some additional payments also made to the sweeper on Eid, festivals etc. Although there are some payments made, there is no regular arrangement for such a system.	■ A mechanism of cross subsidy develops. ■ Perveen kept a strong contact with other residents and the sweeper, as she was available in the area. ■ Payments are not strictly considered as fees against a service.
■ According to Perveen, the system could be improved if the sweeper was provided with proper	

Box 16. Perveen's programme in Charaon Nagar, Dhaka *(continued)*

Narrative   **Commentary**

equipment, such as tri-cycles etc.
She does not know who is the
supervisor or the inspector for the
city corporation in this area.
Recently, they have closer contact
with the Ward Commissioner in the
area. This system is now 5 to 6
months old.

**Box 17. Summary of findings from the interviews of sweepers
in Faisalabad**

Basic information
- A total of 30 semi-structured interviews were conducted in different areas of Faisalabad using a check list. The respondents were both private and municipal, both male and female.

Key findings
- Municipal sanitary sweepers jobs are dominated by Christian Punjabi sweepers belonging to different castes. In a number of cases, the municipal sweeping job is shared by more than one family member. The work is also inherited from an older family member to a younger one.

- Most of the sweepers know each other, support each other and live in the same residential area. This provides a strong relationship among sweepers and they act as a strong occupational group and caste group.

- A number of sweepers would like to educate their children and do not want them to join the sweeping work, which they see as stigmatising. However, a considerable number of sweepers are still looking for sweepers' jobs in the FMC for their son or daughters. This is an indication of an upward mobility in sweepers groups, but there is always a considerable number of poor available to take up the job.

- Municipal jobs provide a lot of security and flexibility to sweepers:

**Box 17. Summary of findings from the interviews of sweepers
in Faisalabad (continued)**

---

1. As a single occupational group, they feel a collective security, which isimportant since Christian Punjabi is a minority group in a predominantly Muslim country.

2. They do not have to interact with many people. They only deal with sanitary inspectors and supervisors.

3. They have long term life security in the form of negotiating jobs for their wives, sons or daughters. There is the security of a pension and options are available for early retirement.

4. Flexibility of working hours, once negotiation is done with supervisor.

5. Opportunities to do private waste collection and other jobs.

6. Opportunities to supplement their income through tips, gifts etc. and allowances on ceremonies, special days etc.

7. Overall security because of the status of being attached to a government organisation.

8. Work load is reasonable.

■ Most of the conflicts among sweepers are resolved through recognised local leaders (who appear non-political). Sweepers living in the same locality identify names of those 'respected' people.

■ The relationship between sweepers and sanitary supervisors and inspectors is interesting. In fact, sweepers only deal with supervisors/inspectors for all their job related problems. As the field representative of FMC they supervise sweepers' work and negotiate all benefits and supports for them from the municipal corporation. It is a two way exchange of support. Most of the sweepers are happy with this arrangement. Various components of this arrangement are as follows:

Box 17. Summary of findings from the interviews of sweepers in Faisalabad (continued)

Sanitary Supervisor/Inspectors	Sweepers
■ Sanitary supervisor marks sweeper's attendance and prepares his salary bill. Sweepers receive their salaries as cash from sanitary supervisor/inspectors.	■ Assist others in getting an appointment in the municipal corporation sometimes in return for a sum of money.
■ Sanitary inspector is also responsible for the proper delivery of service from sweepers. To ensure that the sweeper is present in the field.	■ Sweepers pay a regular amount of Rs 200 to 300 per month to sanitary supervisor/ inspectors.
■ To unofficially allow sweeper to undertake private waste collection jobs.	■ If sweepers do not want to attend their duty area, they need to pay half of the salary to sanitary supervisor or inspector.
■ To allow sweeper for leave and arrange a replacement, if he/she is going for a longer duration.	■ If sweepers want to work only for half day, they need to pay Rs 500 per month to sanitary inspector or supervisor. Similarly, there are rates for leave, for two days' leave they have to pay Rs 50 and for five days' leave Rs 100.
■ To recommend the case for sweepers' transfer if he is not happy with his work.	■ If sweepers want to take early retirement with or without a replacement appointment of a son or daughter, they have to pay Rs 25000 to 50000.
■ Allow sweepers to complete work in a shorter time instead of official duty time of 5:30 a.m to 10:00 a.m and 1:30 p.m to 4:30 p.m.	■ Sweepers are expected to obey instructions from sanitary supervisor/inspectors.
■ When councillors are working, they also share the responsibilities of monitoring and supervision with sanitary supervisors and inspectors.	■ Sweepers obey councillor's instructions in terms of duties and attending complaints.

■ Sweepers' arrangements with sanitary inspector (primary collection organizations) may be efficient and decentralised sub-groups within the large so-called in-efficient and corrupt organizations.

■ Sweepers are always interested in additional income along with the security of a municipal job. However, compared with private sweepers, they are not interested in facing risks.

Box 17. Summary of findings from the interviews of sweepers in Faisalabad (continued)

■ Power structures play an important role in the waste management structure. Whoever holds the power tries to exchange money out of it. There are ownership and informal activities. Sweepers at the transfer stations do not allow private sweepers to dispose of waste at those points unless they pay some money.

■ Sweepers admit that they perform house to house collection of waste and charge money from the households. Details of the house to house collection and transaction of money and goods is given in the table below:

Case no.	Status	Sex	Area description	Private work	Monetary payments	Other payments
1	Permanent Municipal	Male	Shadab Colony, Lower Middle	None	None	None
2	Permanent Municipal	Male	Mustafabad, near Islamnagar, Low income	Primary Coll. from 30 houses	Rs 10-20 per house per week	Task based payments
3	Permanent Municipal	Female	Gulshan Colony, Higher Middle Income	None	None	None
4	Temporary Municipal	Female	Jail Main Road about 0.75 km	In high income Civil lines area	Rs 400 per month	Not mentioned
5	Permanent Municipal	Male	Shadab Colony, Lower Middle	Prim. Coll. 200 houses	20 per house, give 5% to Society	Separate waste gets Rs 100 per week
6	Permanent Municipal	Male		Prim. Coll. 250 houses	Rs 5 - 10 per house per month	Separate paper etc. earn Rs 30 to 40 per day Assists his brother in prim. coll. in the afternoon
7	Private	Male	Shadab Colony, Lower Middle	Prim. Coll. 50 houses	Rs 20 per house per month	Old clothes, food etc. as gifts
8	Permanent Municipal	Male		Prim. Coll. from 100 houses	Rs 2 per house per week	Old clothes, food etc. as gifts Separate plastics, bottles, papers etc. Cleaning one school after his duty and get Rs 300 per month

Box 17. Summary of findings from the interviews of sweepers in Faisalabad (continued)

Case no.	Status	Sex	Area description	Private work	Monetary payments	Other payments
9	Private	Male	Ali Housing Lower Middle	Prim. Coll. from 135 houses	Rs 25 per house per month Rs 150 from buffaloes keepers	Separates and sells waste give Rs 10 to 15 per daily
10	Private	Male	Shiekh Colony Lower Middle	Prim. Coll. from 80 houses	Rs 20 to 25 for domestic waste collection	Gets extra money for additional jobs Gets food, clothes, cash etc from the households
11	Temporary Municipal	Male	Muslim Town Higher Middle (duty area is grain market)	Prim. Coll. from 120 houses	Rs 30 as minimum charges per house per month	Some people pay Rs 50 per month Separate glass, paper etc.
12	Temporary Municipal	Male	Near Civil Lines Higher Middle Income	Prim. Coll. from 80 houses in the area.	Rs 2 to 10 per week per house	Other private jobs to earn extra money
13	Permanent Municipal	Male		Private work in WAPDA's office	Earn Rs 1100 extra from two private jobs	
14	Permanent Municipal	Male	Bhole di Jhugi Roads and Shops	Waste from shops	Variable amounts from shops	
15	Permanent Municipal	Male	Near Jhal Khanuwana Roads and Shops	Different types of works to earn extra income	Occasional payments from shops	
16	Permanent Municipal	Male	Hajveri Town	Prim. Coll from 1000 houses	Rs 2 to 3 per week per house	Separate re-saleables earn 100 per week Special payments on marriages and festivals
17	Permanent Municipal	Male		Prim. Coll. from 150 houses	Rs 2 to 5 per week or Rs 10 to 15 per month	Special payments on marriages and festivals

Box 17. Summary of findings from the interviews of sweepers in Faisalabad (continued)

Case no.	Status	Sex	Area description	Private work	Monetary payments	Other payments
18	Permanent Municipal	Female	Maqbool Road Ghausia Chowk			
19	Permanent Municipal	Male		Prim. Coll. from 400 houses	Rs 15 to 20 per house per month	Special payments on marriages and festivals
20	Permanent Municipal	Male	Mansoorabad	Prim. Coll. from 100 houses	Rs 10 to 15 per house per month	
21	Permanent Municipal	Male	Abid Shaheed Road Commercial Area	Prim. Coll. from 40 houses	Rs 5 per week per house	Special payments on marriages and festivals
22	Permanent Municipal	Male	D-type colony	Prim. Coll. from 200 houses	Rs 2 to 5 per week or Rs 20 per month	Special payments on marriages and festivals
23	Permanent Municipal	Male	D-type colony	Prim. Coll. from 40 to 50 houses	Rs 2 to 10 per week	Special payments on marriages and festivals
24	Permanent Municipal	Male	D-type colony Commercial area	Prim. Coll. from 50 shops	Rs 20 to 30 per shop per month	
25	Permanent Municipal	Male	Gulberg area	Prim. Coll. from 90 houses	Rs 10 to 15 per house per month	Special payments on marriages and festivals
26	Permanent Municipal	Male				
27	Municipal Retired	Male	Gulistan Colony with his friend	Prim. Coll. from 200 houses with his friend and wife	Rs 20 per house per month	Special payments on marriages and festivals
28	Permanent Municipal	Female				
29	Permanent Municipal	Female	Mansoorabad			
30	Permanent Municipal	Male	Street 4 and 5?	Prim. Coll from 50 houses	Rs 10 per house per month	Special payments on marriages and festivals

Box 18. Anonymous , a sweeper working with Faisalabad Municipal Corporation (FMC)

Narrative	Commentary
■ He lives in a Christian colony (Nasarat Colony). It is a low-income area. Most of the residents are daily workers. There are about 12 men/women working as sanitary workers with the municipal corporation. Christianity is the strongest unit which bonds them together. There are sub-castes among Christians but the concept of leadership is there and they rely on their leaders for the resolution of conflicts. One Sanitary Inspector also lives there. All the basic facilities such as sewers, metalled roads, electricity, telephone etc. are also available, since they have their own elected representative, who gets special grants for the development of their community.	■ The area is well served with all the basic facilities. ■ Indicators of a close-knit and cohesive community. ■ Mechanism for conflict resolution exists.
■ The supervisor marks their daily attendance at a designated place. If the sweepers need leave on certain days, they have to give the supervisor Rs 200-300 depending on the requirements. Similarly, in order to achieve some mutual settlement such as change in work schedule, the sweepers have to pay. Although their working hours are officially from 5-10 am and then 2-4 pm, he may work from 7-2 pm with a mutual verbal understanding with the supervisor which is called a 'good relation-ship'. The supervisor plays an important role in checking the work of sweepers and he is also a link between the workers and the department.	■ Supervisor is the only link between sweepers and municipal corpora-tion. ■ Supervisor decides the working principles in practice. ■ There is a charge for any change in work schedule etc.
■ His duty area is Shadab colony which is not a fully developed area. He does not collect waste from the houses but occasionally works for different households who compen-sate him with payments in kind e.g clothes, food etc.	■ Private work by the sweeper is practised. ■ Payments are not only in the form of money.

Box 19. Anonymous, a female sweeper working with Faisalabad Municipal Corporation (FMC)

Narrative

- She lives in Gole Bhatta near the fish farms. It is a recognised Katchi Abadi and all the residents have legal rights. It comprises of 436 Allotments (Plots). At least one person per household is employed with FMC or WASA as a sanitary worker. Other than electricity, there are no facilities available in the area. This colony has two main bazaars. The remaining streets are quite narrow, about 3-6 feet wide. Muslims and Christians are living amicably together. There are about 100 Christian families who are all related to each other. They have their own social leader from the same locality who resolves social conflicts.

- Her two sons are working at a vehicle service station and are getting Rs. 400 per month each. One son has just started learning the job of a motor mechanic and is getting a small allowance from the owner of the shop. She runs/ manages her family. She is getting Rs.2400 per month as salary from the FMC. She got the job in FMC when her mother in law retired from the service. She took on the job because she needed the money. She is strongly against this profession due to the low status and low salary. She does not want to send her children into this profession.

- She explained that although she is not happy with the job, there are advantages to serving in a regular government job. e.g. one gets a lump sum amount at the end i.e. pension and also a monthly leave entitlement and some flexibility in duty hours.

- She explained that the inspectors/ supervisors are very important for the sweepers. According to her,

Commentary

- The area is well served with a few basic facilities.

- Indicators of a close-knit and cohesive community living at the same place.

- Mechanism for conflict resolution exists.

- Indication of an upward mobility among sweepers.

- At the same time sweepers also appreciate the benefits of a regular government job.

- Supervisor is the only link between sweepers and municipal corporation.

Box 19. Anonymous, a female sweeper working with Faisalabad Municipal Corporation (FMC) *(continued)*

Narrative	Commentary
they manage the sweepers' duties and without them the system cannot function. She does not need to pay anybody as she performs her duty according to the given schedule. She has never visited the FMC's office as her needs/problems are addressed at the level of the Sanitary Inspectors. She expresses her concern that the FMC is no longer employing female sweepers as they believe that females cannot work properly due to their maternal duties.	■ Supervisor decides the working principles in practice. ■ She has no organisational links with FMC.
■ She is serving in municipal ward number 38 i.e. Gulshan colony. This is a high-income area with a metalled road and is served by sewerage facilities as well. According to her, FMC gave her a comparatively small area for duty. She is not involved in the waste collection from the houses (private work). Her duty is to sweep the roads and dispose of the collected waste to the filth depot (transfer points). She mentioned that there are private waste collectors working in the area. She has to come to the filth depot situated near Gulberg police station, which is about 1 km from her duty area. Her actual duty timings are from 5.30 am - 10 am and from 1.30 pm - 4.30 pm. She normally serves from 6.00 am - 1.00 pm instead. She has to mark her attendance at 10.30 am and 1.30 pm. Sunday is the day off. They can also take two days' leave in a month. For the improvement of the system, she suggested that transfer stations should be nearer, because at present they have to go a long distance with the handcarts, which are not suitable. The FMC has not provided her with a handcart or other tools and at present two people are sharing one hand cart. They do not receive any maintenance costs from the FMC for the handcarts.	■ The municipal sweepers do not practise private work. ■ No handcart and tools are provided by FMC and there is no system of repair and maintenance.

Box 20. Summary of findings from the interviews of sweepers in Dhaka

Basic information

■ A total of 41 semi-structured interviews were conducted in different areas of Dhaka.

■ The distribution of private and municipal sweepers and their gender division is as follows:

Key findings

■ In Dhaka, a large proportion of sweepers are working on daily wages. The salaries and benefits for daily wage sweepers are low compared to permanent municipal sweepers, although there is always a hope that once in the system, they will ultimately become a permanent employee.

■ Municipal sanitary sweepers' jobs are distributed among migrated Hindu and Muslim sweepers with a few Christians who belong to different castes. In a number of cases, the municipal sweeping job is shared by more than one family member. The work is also passed on from an older family member to a younger one.

■ Most of the sweepers know each other, support each other and live in the same residential area. This provides a strong relationship among sweepers and they act as a strong occupational group.

■ There are few opportunities for sweepers to get education for their children. There are few trends for upward mobility, while there is strong competition for jobs between Hindu and Muslim sweepers.

■ Municipal job provides a lot of security and flexibility to sweepers:

1. Sweepers in Dhaka are no longer a single occupational group as other groups are entering. However Hindu sweepers still feel a collective security, which is important since as Hindus are a minority group in Bangladesh.

2. There is a certain minimum level of interaction with Dhaka City Corporation as they actually receive some consumables and equipment from them. Similarly, their involvement is greater than those in Faisalabad. For their work related problems, they still deal with the sanitary inspector or supervisors.

Box 20. Summary of findings from the interviews of sweepers in Dhaka *(continued)*

3. They have long term life security in the form of negotiating jobs for their wives, sons or daughters. There is the security of a pension and other options are available for early retirement.

4. Working hours are flexible after negotiation with supervisor. There are many opportunities to do private waste collection and other jobs and opportunities to supplement their income through tips, gifts etc.

5. Overall security exists because of the status of being attached to a government organisation.

6. Work load is reasonable and there are allowances on ceremonies, special days etc.

■ Most of the conflicts among sweepers are resolved through recognised local leaders (who appear non-political). Sweepers living in the same locality identify names of those 'respected' people.

■ In Dhaka a number of sweepers also left their municipal jobs to work in middle eastern countries for higher wages. Upon their return to Dhaka, they started the same work either as a daily wage sweeper or in a private job. The extra income from middle eastern jobs helped them to build certain assets.

■ The sweepers' relationship with sanitary supervisors and inspectors is an interesting one and very similar to Faisalabad. As the field representatives of DCC, they supervise the sweepers' work and negotiate all benefits and support for them from municipal corporation. Sweepers have to pay fixed amounts of money to supervisors to acquire favours. A number of supervisors expressed their resentment of such practices.

■ Sweepers dislike paying supervisors, but accept their importance in working. They think that supervisors also take important decisions if there is conflict in the working area, problems from fellow sweepers etc.

Box 21. Anonymous, key informant interview with a sweeper in Dhaka

Narrative

- He is a resident of Waris Sweepers Colony (Dhangot), by birth. The area is has been inhabited since the colonial period (before 1947). He explained that the 'Britis' (British) government provided this place and sweepers have lived in this area since then. Compared with other countries, he feels that they have not been provided with proper facilities.

- He said that his forefathers were invited from India to clean this country by the British, but now local 'Bangalee' sweepers are entering this profession and it is even more difficult to find a job because of the competition. He works as a daily wage sweeper, i.e. if there is no work, there is no pay. He feels that this is a very low status job.

- His father was working in the city corporation, but he was retrenched (locally known as 'Chahtai'). His father was also working on the daily basis of 'no work no pay', this is called 'ad-hoc' or 'daily wages' without the facilities and allowances of the permanent job, such as increments, allowances, provident fund, service record etc. He has been working on this basis for the last nine years. He is now about 25 years of age.

- All his brothers and sisters are younger than him. His mother is also working in DCC on an ad-hoc basis. His brother goes to a school, which is established by an NGO, 'Food For Hunger'. According to him, the NGO is doing some useful work and has been assisting sweepers for the last 15 years. His hopes to educate his brother and sisters and prevent them from joining sweeping work.

- There are about 250 houses in his residential area, which are

Commentary

- Indication of an old and established settlement.

- Sweepers living at the same place, sign of a cohesive colony with strong social networks.

- Clear signs of an emerging competition with the Muslim sweepers.

- The job status as well as income deteriorated with time.

- Further endorsement of problems of ad-hoc appointments.

- Evidence of long term work as daily wage sweepers and fear of competition.

- Evidences of upward mobility but at a slow rate.

- Availability of means to gain upward mobility.

- High population density but valid need to live at the same place.

**Box 21. Anonymous, key informant interview with a sweeper in Dhaka
(continued)**

Narrative	Commentary
occupied by more than 350 families, since a number of houses have been sub-divided. There are common lavatories on two sides; these are maintained by the community. There are two 'hauz' (storage tanks) for the supply of water. Sweepers are not the owners of these houses, but are living there.	■ Signs of cohesive community.
■ He spoke about the possibility that the ad-hoc service may be made regular at some stage. He thinks that there is a system of bribe (ghose), which works everywhere. To get an ad-hoc appointment, which means to get a place to live, it is necessary to pay an amount of Tk 20,000.	■ Indication of limited or no opportunities for sweepers to work in other areas. ■ Payment for appointments is a practice similar to what was observed in Faisalabad.
■ He is a drain cleaning sweeper. Once he finishes his work, the Conservancy Inspector (CI) checks it and he marks the attendance. According to him, there are very few households in this city who like a sweeper to come and collect their waste in return for some payment. In most of the areas, residents throw it away themselves. In some areas, however, if residents call sweepers to collect waste regularly, the sweeper can do it, provided he/she is paid for the service. This service is charged for but the mode of payment is not fixed and will depend upon the relationship with the household. He remarked 'could do this work for love ('mohabbat')'. The transaction may be tea, sometimes 5 Taka or just love.	■ Low need for a primary collection service, although this is gradually on the rise. ■ The charges could be in the form of money or payment in kind.
■ He was aware of the Kolabaghan system (Box 14). He was informed that the municipal sweepers participate in the programme. He feels that the programme may not be successful, since people will not pay. Residents will throw the waste in the street, but will not give it to	■ Poor trust with residents. ■ Sweepers like to see public sector development and may be a part of it as it develops. ■ Sweepers are threatened by higher profits of the programme organiser.

Box 21. Anonymous, key informant interview with a sweeper in Dhaka *(continued)*

Narrative	Commentary
the sweeper. He feels that the major profit is taken by the capitalist (the person who owns the vehicle and pays the salaries), however, an additional salary of Tk 1200 is a major benefit to the sweeper.	
■ In order to acquire a job in the city corporation, a sweeper has to pay and the sweepers usually take loans from someone in order to acquire a job. The loans attract interest, which sweepers need to return in instalments. There are a number of money lenders in their community and outside the community. A number of them are also from the same caste (biradari).	■ There is still a demand and a price for a sweepers' job. ■ Payments for the job are also in the vested interest of moneylenders.
■ When, asked if Conservancy Inspectors (CIs) also lend money on interest, he replied that *'Yae Sala Log Bara Harami Hay'* (means these people are very corrupt). The CIs charge 'Dastoori' from municipal sweepers. The current rate of Dastoori is between 100 to 200 Tk per month and all the sweepers pay that amount regularly (*'Saaab log datay hein'*). This means that everybody pays. According to him, sweepers cannot get away without paying. Inspectors also log attendance on a daily basis.	■ Clear dependency on sanitary inspectors. ■ Regular payments to inspectors. ■ Additional payments for additional favours, a system similar to Faisalabad.
■ Hand carts etc. are repaired well by the city corporation. When asked about the practice of transfer of collection rights, he said, we could transfer the area among those who are employed by municipal corporation. We could also pay (bribe) CIs for transferring the sweeper to other areas. He further explained the practice of transferring collection rights. He said that such practices are there, but payments are not involved. [in cities sweepers exchange private work for agreed payments]	■ Municipal system of hand cart repair and maintenance still working.

Box 21. Anonymous, key informant interview with a sweeper in Dhaka *(continued)*

Narrative	Commentary
■ Part-time work for sanitary sweepers (those who clean drains) does not guarantee regular payment. However, if a drain is blocked, they charge a certain amount of money from the household to clear it.	■ Potential for other regular incomes.
■ In cases of conflict, they have Sardars (elders) who can resolve the problem. They are not necessarily members of punchayat committee but most of them accept their advice. In cases when the elders could not resolve and in the event of a very serious crime like theft or murder, then the police are involved, but this costs a lot of money for both parties. On the mutual support system, people normally help, particularly those who are close relations. They don't have a mutual saving system, but pool money in a *Qistee.* In this system, the participating members, pool a certain amount of money every month and different participant receive it in rotation. When he was asked about the Grameen Bank, he said that they need security which may be in the form of a land or a house etc. In comparison, local money lenders do not need security. We have no property which we could use as security.	■ A system of mutual conflict resolution exists. ■ A system of mutual savings also exists. ■ Security against loans is a problem.
■ Sweepers in Dhaka are from South India, they include Talagua, Harijan, Bhom, Chamar and also muslim Banagali.	
■ City corporation does not trust sweepers. If they trust sweepers and give them areas, the system will improve.	■ Sweepers wish to see a revival of municipal corporation with an integral role for sweepers.

Box 22. Anonymous, a female sweeper working with Dhaka City Corporation (DCC)

Narrative

- She is among the regular sweeping staff of DCC, aged 40 and the mother of five children. Three of her daughters are married. She has been working as a road cleaner since she was 12 years old, when she joined as a cleaner with her father. When her father retired from the job, she was appointed as a permanent sweeper. She explained that the conservancy department of DCC considered family members first for the replacement positions.

- Both she and her husband run the family. Her husband earns Tk.1700 and she earns Tk. 1900 per month. Her husband works in a clinic as a sweeper.

- She said that conflicts are rare amongst the neighbours. If any conflicts take place, some selected persons resolve the disputes. Those persons have been selected by the ward commissioner (elected representative of local government) or by the community.

- She is not satisfied with the current job as this type of job is not well accepted by the general public. So she would not like to engage any of her family members in this profession in the future. She feels that the general public does not show them any respect. She even feels that no family will engage her, even as a household servant.

- All sweepers have to pay Tk.100 to their supervisors per month for the protection of their jobs. If she does not pay any money to the supervisors, she is sure that some different type of harassment would be imposed on her. In addition to that, everyone has to pay half of their one-day salary if they are

Commentary

- Other family members help sweepers in their work.

- The sweeping job remains in the family and so forms a caste monopoly.

- Sweepers marry each other. An indicator of a close occupational and caste group.

- A community representation exists for resolution of conflict.

- In the present situation, sweepers think of themselves as a underclass.

- Sweeping work is considered stigmatising.

- With the improvement in socio-economic indicators, there may be a shortage of sweepers.

- Relationship with the supervisors is similar to that in Faisalabad.

- There are fixed payments for any favour.

Box 22. Anonymous, a female sweeper working with Dhaka City Corporation (DCC) *(continued)*

Narrative	Commentary
absent or require leave. She mentioned that this is a regular practice.	
■ When she needs money, she takes a loan from her supervisor. She does not lend money to her supervisor. Supervisors give loans to those sweepers who are more or less financially sound. She feels that without supervisors, the area would not be clean, there would be regular fighting among the sweepers and no one would obey each other. Because sweepers are not educated, the supervisors' role becomes more important .	■ Supervisors help sweepers socially. ■ Sweepers also accept the importance of supervisors for working.
■ There is a big gap between the sweepers and conservancy department (DCC). Usually, the high officials do not speak to them. They are not allowed to talk to their boss directly if any problems arise. They have to solve their problems through union leaders or supervisors.	■ Some basic problems need to be resolved for efficient working of sweepers.
■ The sweepers have a union. They pay Tk.5 each to the union as a monthly subscription. The union leaders are elected through a direct vote of sweepers. Union leaders are supposed to resolve the sweepers' problems related to their job. The union does not provide any financial support to sweepers.	■ Sweepers unions have some role to play and generally sweepers take out membership.
■ She simply sweeps the road and does not collect any waste from households. She does not usually get any extra money either in cash or in kind from any dwellers in the area where she has been working for a long time. She sweeps the road in an area which is located in the old part of Dhaka City. The roads are narrow and densely populated. For cleaning drains, separate cleaners have been	■ Low opportunities for additional income to sweepers. ■ Reasons for paying money to the supervisor are evident.

Box 22. Anonymous, a female sweeper working with Dhaka City Corporation (DCC) *(continued)*

Narrative	Commentary
engaged. Her official duty hours are eight but she actually works for four to five hours. The transfer point is about 100 metres from her working area.	
■ She considers that only the authority (DCC) can develop the improved mechanism for better solid waste collection system. She has no idea about other options.	■ Sweepers have no experience of other options. ■ Like to continue with the same status.
■ She is provided with soap, a broom, a spade, a shovel and a basket for her daily use. All the tools are kept in the ward commissioner's office, except for the soap. DCC bought all those tools and owns them.	■ The sweepers are provided with tools.
■ When asked her opinion of some different ways of working (see Box 25), she said that if the CBO/NGO initiate the programme (option 1) then it will be found that 50% dwellers would not pay regularly but the sweepers will benefit. Their labour will be reduced to remove solid waste. As a result, the programme will not function.	■ Sweepers feel that residents will not pay the charges.
■ Regarding the second option of a large scale private contractor, she feels that with the introduction of such a system those who work regularly and honestly would get more money but those who do not work hard would be out of a job. At present, many sweepers of DCC do not work and draw 50% of their salary with the recommendation of their supervisors.	■ A strong justification to favour privatisation is to eliminate corruption

Box 23. Summary of Findings from the Interviews of Sweepers in Colombo

- A total of 30 semi-structured interviews were conducted with 20 male and ten female sweepers in different areas of Colombo.

Key findings

- In Colombo, a total number of 1500 sweepers serve a population of 0.65 million. Most of the sweepers are permanent employees of the Colombo Municipal Corporation (CMC).

- The municipal sweepers (locally known as labourers) do not belong to a single caste or operate as a single occupational group. They also live in different low income areas with other residents. Neither is there any preference for sweepers sons or daughters to take-up the sweepers job.

- Opportunities are available for sweepers to get education for their children. However, as not many jobs are available in the city, sweepers tend to stay in the same job for a long time.

- Around 50% of responding sweepers admit that they collect waste from the household and charge a monthly payment of Rs 25 to 50 per house.

- Sweepers in Colombo see a need for sanitary inspectors to check their work, however, there is no transaction of money between sweepers and sanitary inspectors. Sweepers have links with other government departments and take out union membership. Some of them are also members of Community Development Council (CDC), which provides another route to take their problems to CMC.

- Though sweepers deny paying any money to sanitary inspectors, they mention sharing extra income from household waste collection with other staff.

- While discussing the possibilities of micro-enterprise development, they like to work with the existing CDCs in low income areas of Colombo.

- Sweepers acquired jobs in CMC through the normal procedure of responding to an advertisement or through local politicians such as area councillors and others. None of the sweepers interviewed mentioned paying to acquire municipal jobs.

- The level of education of sweepers in Colombo is higher compared to sweepers in Dhaka and Faisalabad. Basic education gives sweepers access to many other facilities such as operating their own bank accounts.

Box 24. Key informant interview with two sweepers in Colombo

Narrative

- They live in Kotte Municipal Area in a low income settlement. In their settlement, 10 or 15 other sweepers also reside. They own their houses, as National Housing Development Authority (NHDA) provided the houses. However, there are still many problems regarding infrastructure. There are stand posts for water and communal toilets. Their fathers were not sweepers and some are in business and others are labourers. Their wives do not work but look after the home and family.

- One of the sweepers said that he has three children, all of them going to school. One boy is educated up to level 7 and another up to level 3. Although, they did mention that it is now more expensive to educate children.

- Their work is monitored by a supervisor, who checks attendance twice daily at 7.30 a.m. and at 1.00 p.m.. Their working hours are 7:30 am to 3:00 p.m. They are permanent employees of the municipal corporation and get a total salary of Rs 2900 per month, including all the allowances. They can also get loans from the municipal corporation up to around Rs 7500, re-payable in ten months or five years' time. They also get a festival allowance of Rs 1500. In addition, they get tips from households, ranging from Rs 25 to 50 per month.

- They need to pay some money to their supervisor in one way or another. This may be in the form of gifts, cash etc. Otherwise supervisors will transfer them to other areas. They have no loan systems between supervisor and workers. They do not have any educational or training programme from their office. They are not provided with protective equipment

Commentary

- There is a clearly defined ownership of the house with the help of a government department.

- Sweeping in Sri Lanka does not transfer from one generation to another.

- Sweepers settlements are not isolated from rest of the community.

- Indication of an upward mobility and availability of education to sweepers' children.

- Links with the municipal corporation are well established.

- Sweepers know what their rights are.

- Payments to supervisors do not exist in a commonly accepted form.

- Low status of sweepers and lack of co-operation from households is a problem.

101

Box 24. Key informant interview with two sweepers in Colombo
 (continued)

Narrative	Commentary
such as boots, hats, rain coats etc. They use a Savala (fork) provided by the government. They are also given carts, but these are very heavy and difficult to push when fully loaded. When the cart needs repairing, they tell the supervisor, who refers it to the maintenance officer/branch. They are low paid and have little incentive to work. They provide a service but the public do not respect and praise them.	
■ Householders are not educated to give rubbish to the collector at a certain time and they throw it into the street. People always think that waste collection is the job of a municipal sweeper and not a service for which they have to pay. In the rainy season, it is very difficult for the sweepers to work as they do not have raincoats etc. Also the garbage becomes very heavy and smells. They dislike the container system, since it is difficult to dispose of waste into them	■ There is a dependency on the municipal corporation. ■ Primary collection may be a low priority.
■ They collect waste from some areas and charge money for the service. This is an informal practice which their supervisor does not know about. If he did know he may transfer them or ask for some money. If this system could be formalised, they would like to do some private work.	■ They already do private work on an informal basis and without the knowledge of their supervisor. ■ They would like to do private work in addition to the municipal work.
■ They have three categories of sweepers, sweeper, drainage sweeper and road sweeper. Sweepers collect waste from the houses, the drainage sweeper cleans drains and the road sweepers sweep the road.	■ Such categorisation is useful and does not exist in any other city of South Asia.
■ Many women are working as road sweepers. Both the respondents were sweepers. There is a Union in	■ Participation in the union is high.

Box 24. Key informant interview with two sweepers in Colombo *(continued)*

Narrative	Commentary
their office and all members pay Rs 45 per month to that union. About 90% of sweepers are union members. The benefit is if someone dies in the family, they get Rs 3500 and tents, chairs, tables etc. and a flower bouquet. Once a year they also organise a sports festival.	
■ They have a pension which they receive after retirement. They work six days per week (not Sundays). If they work on Sundays, they get overtime. Temporary sweepers have only 21 days to work and no overtime and other allowances. They have no saving systems, since their salaries are so low. They spend all the money they earn.	
■ When they were asked about the difference between the public and private sweeper, they mentioned that they like public sector jobs, because of loans, gratuities, security of job etc. If a private firm provides the same security of job, they would prefer to work under that organisation.	■ Sweepers like the secure jobs of public sector agencies.
■ In case of minor conflicts, normally neighbours intervene and solve the problem. If the neighbours cannot resolve the problem then they go to the police. The elders do not intervene in such cases. There is also no system of mutual support, but if they need money they can borrow it from the Kotte municipal corporation.	■ A system of conflict resolution exists.

Box 25. Sweepers' opinions of different options in the three cities

Sweepers were given different options to choose the best one for their future. The following options were proposed:

1) Area based organisations and intermediaries, hiring sweepers and paying their salaries.

2) Large scale private organisations appointed by the metropolitan corporation, hiring and paying sweepers directly.

3) Sweepers will form micro-enterprises, which is a small scale waste collection company.

4) Continue with the same system.

The number of sweepers who gave favourable opinion on a certain option are given below:

Options	Faisalabad	Colombo	Dhaka
Option 1 (CBOs)	25%	0%	3%
Option 2 (Contractor)	0%	0%	13%
Option 3 (micro-enterprise)	4%	27%	18%
Option 4 (Present System)	64%	73%	59%
No opinion/others	7%	0%	8%

The majority of sweepers would like to continue with the present system (Option 4) of government jobs as they perceive more security and benefits with it. On the other hand, they have no experience of any other system and have not seen in the past any changes which have benefitted the sweepers' community. This lack of experience restricts their ability to choose an option representing only what they have experienced. For example, in Colombo, 27% of sweepers have shown interest in the idea of forming micro-enterprises; the main reason could perhaps be the comparatively efficient institutions, with less corruption. In addition, sweepers have seen some successful interventions by the government in housing and other sectors, which really benefitted the poor. Similarly, in Faisalabad 25% of sweepers favour the option of hiring and paying sweepers through community-based organisations, as they have witnessed some systems operating. However, they want to participate in such a system in addition to their municipal jobs and see it as an opportunity to do extra work and earn a supplementary income. In this way, sweepers could enjoy the security of a municipal job and gain official recognition of their private work. Overall, it is evident that sweepers would like to continue with the present system and their trust in any future change will depend upon their confidence in the institutions who will bring about these changes.

Box 26. Summary of findings from the interviews of municipal sanitary inspectors in Faisalabad

Basic information

- Eight sanitary inspectors and two sanitary supervisors were interviewed, all of them male.

- All the sanitary inspectors have completed a one year diploma in Community Medicine, although their basic qualification varies.

- All sanitary inspectors look after one or two supervisors and between 40 to 60 sweepers in their assigned area.

Key findings

- All the sanitary inspectors express a feeling of ownership for their staff and area. For example, most of them claim that they want to retain good workers and help them in getting leave and allowances.

- All the sanitary inspectors have delegated powers of field supervision and attendance to sanitary supervisors or to a sanitary worker called 'Danda Supervisor' (supervisor with a baton). Danda supervisor is an ordinary sweeper with more powers.

- Official duties of sanitary inspectors also include dealing with slaughter houses, encroachments, hygienic condition and licenses of food shops, hotels and restaurants.

- In most cases sanitary supervisors check attendance of sanitary workers, twice a day: once at 10:00 am and again at 1.30 pm. There are fixed places to mark attendance but some sanitary supervisors do not force their workers to come for the attendance, particularly women (who could not ride a bike or a donkey cart). The attendance point is used to allocate special duties, dealing with complaints and assigning 'Wigar' for absentees.

- Transfer of sweepers to other areas has been identified as the second level of punishment after verbal warning (this shows sweepers' interest in the area). The third level of punishment is to report the case to the Health Officer for an explanation. Punishing and firing of a sanitary worker is an extremely lengthy procedure, which is normally avoided. Only the city mayor or administrator has the power to sack a sanitary worker or discontinue his pay.

Box 26. Summary of findings from the interviews of municipal sanitary inspectors in Faisalabad (continued)

- The responding inspectors admit that the distribution of sweepers in each ward is not based on any criteria of population or area, but only on the political pressure and other reasons such as income opportunities for sweepers.

- Sanitary inspectors are positive about the private practices of house to house collection by sweepers. They also admit that about 50% of sweepers keep their own donkey carts, to save time, help them in private works etc.

- Sanitary inspectors are not in favour of the involvement of Community Based Organisations (CBOs), they feel that they will soon start 'black-mailing' municipal staff. The CBOs also pressurise sanitary supervisors to transfer more manpower to their areas. They also interfere in payments to sweepers and other businesses.

- Most of the sanitary inspectors admit that they give loans to reliable sweepers in the range of Rs 50 to 500. The loan is to be returned on the pay day. If inspectors do not get it on the pay day, sweepers may not return it at all.

- Most of the sanitary inspectors and supervisors give a list of major constraints in the current waste management, this includes:

1. Shortage of staff;

2. Shortage of equipment;

3. No system of maintenance;

4. Poor secondary collection;

5. Shortage and poor locations of filth depots;

6. Poor co-ordination; and,

7. Poor enforcement of law.

- If CBOs are going to hire private (self employed) sweepers for the collection of household waste, the municipal sweepers will not allow them to dispose of rubbish at the 'official' transfer points unless he gets a 'Parchee' (written permission) from the sanitary inspector of the area.

Box 26. Summary of findings from the interviews of municipal sanitary inspectors in Faisalabad *(continued)*

- All the supervisors feel that hiring private sweepers is not an ideal option, since they are not reliable and may run away with money.

- Elected councillors take charge of looking after sweepers if they are in their seats.

- To get an appointment as a municipal supervisor, one needs a minimum qualification of 10 levels, plus an 'approach' and a payment of Rs 20,000 to 30,000 [some supervisors claim this amount as Rs 50,000].

- There are a number of additional benefits for sweepers in the government service:

- Upto Rs 3500 welfare fund for marriage;

- Rs 10,000 to 30,000 loan for the construction of house; and,

- Rs 500, welfare fund for funeral.

- Example of Noor-ul-Amin Society has been mentioned as a positive example, since sweepers (sanitary workers) were handed over to the Society, they marked attendance and equipment was provided by the Society. However, due to political influence sweepers were taken back from the Society.

Box 27. Summary of findings from the interviews of municipal sanitary inspectors in Dhaka and Colombo

- A total of eight interviews were conducted with sanitary inspectors (locally known as conservancy inspector) of Dhaka City Corporation (DCC) and ten interviews were conducted in Colombo with sanitary inspectors (locally known as Overseers).

- In both sets of interviews, the inspectors gave the 'official version' of what they do and their responsibilities. They identify the community's lack of awareness, shortage of communal bins and trucks as the main problems.

- Sanitary inspector level is the stage from where the official stream in solid waste management actually starts.

Box 28. Key points from brainstorming workshop in Faisalabad with sanitary inspectors and supervisors

A brainstorming workshop was organised on Sunday, the 3rd November, 1996 with the Sanitary Inspectors of FMC. The Chief Medical Officers of Health, Faisalabad, nominated 20 inspectors to attend the workshop. The participants also include inspectors from the DFID funded Faisalabad Area Upgrading Project (FAUP) areas.

Under one of the themes of discussions, the concept of community-based organisations and the role of micro-enterprises were explained to the inspectors. The concept of community-based primary collection system which FAUP intends to support was also explained. The proposed roles of sweepers, community-based organisations and FAUP were clarified. The discussion was then opened to talk through the benefits, problems and constraints of the proposed activity. The section below gives a narrative summary of the discussion with author's comments.

Narrative	Commentary
■ More community involvement may create problems for sweepers since MPCOs and the community may start misusing municipal sweepers for their private works.	■ Inspectors may not like to share authority. ■ Inspectors have no trust over MPCOs. ■ Some form of contract may help.
■ Political influence in FMC may create problems for the community-based systems, since pressure from politicians causes unjustified distribution of sweepers.	■ Political will is necessary for any change. ■ Large-scale changes are required to sustain any change.
■ There is a need to create overall awareness and health education in communities. The community must be educated about keeping waste in bins and giving it to sweepers at a proper time. They must not dispose of waste on streets once the collection round has been completed.	■ This is extremely important and could be done by community based organisation. ■ Important for a smooth working relationship with the municipal corporation.
■ The MPCO should have a structure and the list and name of the contact person must be provided to the FMC and the respective sanitary inspector. This will help in developing a sustainable partnership.	

Box 28. Key points from brainstorming workshop in Faisalabad with sanitary inspectors and supervisors *(continued)*

Narrative	Commentary
■ We must be careful about the internal grouping within the communities.	
■ Sweepers do not get any hand tools from FMC and there is also a shortage of handcarts. FAUP and MPCOs could provide equipment and carts to the sweepers. Sweepers would carry out the repair and maintenance of hand equipment and carts. If a sweeper is leaving an area, the new sweeper could borrow the equipment from MPCO. For example, Ayub Welfare Society has provided two donkey carts to the sweeper. The repair and maintenance of the cart is the responsibility of the sweeper. According to the sanitary inspector, this system has increased sweepers' productivity and now he could also remove construction debris, which is difficult to collect with the existing hand cart. The Society also pays additional money to the sweeper.	■ External support is important and must be arranged.
■ Another example is from Noor-ul-Amin Society (Bihari Tanzeem), which only provided the equipment to the sweeper. Similarly some work has been done through Gulberg Welfare Society near Baghdadi Mosque Park.	
■ MPCO could invite the sanitary inspector and the sweeper to their monthly meeting. FAUP could check that the sweeper is not being exploited by the MPCO.	
■ Payments to sanitary workers is not an issue and could be justified on the following basis: Collection of the household waste is not the responsibility of the municipal sweeper, additional payments must be made for extra work and sweeper could involve their	■ Sanitary inspectors justify payments to sweepers for additional work.

Box 28. Key points from brainstorming workshop in Faisalabad with sanitary inspectors and supervisors (*continued*)

Narrative	**Commentary**
relatives for the collection work. Sanitary supervisor does not see additional income to sweepers as an issue.	
■ If sweepers do not see additional income from the area, they leave the area in search of more lucrative jobs/opportunities.	■ A constraint to extend services to low income areas.

Box 29. Key points from brainstorming workshop in Dhaka with sanitary inspectors and supervisors

The workshop was arranged in Collaboration with ICDDR,B and was conducted in the new city corporation building, Dhaka. Most of the participants were enthusiastic and ready for the workshop, which is reflected in the discussion throughout the workshop.

The concept of community participation in solid waste management was explained. Participants were asked to describe the benefits and problems of different theme topics. The term 'no participation' was defined in terms of just disposing of waste in the street. Formation of clubs, NGOs etc. is also a form of community participation. Some examples of problems associated with the participation were also explained.

Narrative	**Commentary**
■ Elected Ward Commissioner's system has been perceived as a form of community participation from participants, since there are 90 Wards in Dhaka and each ward is represented by a Commissioner. Participants suggested that, if we do not strengthen the Ward system, the problem of true representation will arise. The Ward Commissioner is a member of the board at DCC, all the supervision staff work under the direction of the Ward Commissioner. In each Ward, the population is generally	■ Similar to Faisalabad, the municipal staff like to see the development of existing system. ■ The concept mentioned here is very different from what is generally perceived by donors and NGOs.

Box 29. Key points from brainstorming workshop in Dhaka with sanitary inspectors and supervisors *(continued)*

Narrative	Commentary
100, 000 (different population figures were mentioned about the size of each ward). It was mentioned that only a few wards have a population in excess of 100,000.	
■ In addition, the sweepers get their salary upon the signature of Ward Commissioner. On the other hand, it is important that community participation increases and other models are tested. At present, we do not have many examples, only in Kalabogan area, through Mr Mahbub Ahsan, there is a participatory project.	■ Sanitary inspectors know about the Kolabaghan programme (Box 14). ■ The mayor considers solid waste management as an important area for consideration.
■ Each Ward Commissioner has several (about eight) standing committees under him, one for conservancy, but there is no standing committee on solid waste or sanitation. Conservancy is looked after by the Mayor himself (earlier he said that there are Ward Commissioners in the standing Committees). The Mayor also appointed two co-ordinators to look after inter-city (city level) management. Every month there is a meeting of co-ordinating officers with Ward Commissioners.	■ Need for a more co-ordinated approach at ward level.
■ Small clubs, NGOs etc. could assist the Ward Commissioner, but there is a risk of conflict between them and the Ward Commissioner on the sharing of power and political influences. The risk of conflict could be reduced through more communication and mutual trust. There are problems in every task but they could be controlled. At the neighbourhood level, there should be more co-ordination between clubs, conservancy inspectors (CIs), Ward Commissioners and the general public.	■ The concept of service and payments does not exist.

Box 29. Key points from brainstorming workshop in Dhaka with sanitary inspectors and supervisors *(continued)*

Narrative

- Since waste management is a job of 'haya alal falah' (a welfare work with no reward) so each and every person could be involved. In any form of community participation there is usually great success as we saw in Kolabagan area. The City Corporation could also start an effective system, similar to Kolabagan, however the community is reluctant to pay the government representatives etc. The Community Participants could be seen in four or five areas, educational materials, payment of fees, co-operation with the municipal system etc.

- While discussing the idea of small scale contractors, one of the participants mentioned that the major problem is the replacement of the area sweepers. Since sweepers understand the area well and they know each and every door they must be present in the area. Sweepers also perform the cleaning of drains in front of every house, sweeping of streets etc. Contractors will 'blackmail' public before they clean their front, ask for more money etc. It is better that sweepers should continue in their areas.

- On the point of privatisation, the supervisory staff does not have any say. The policy comes from the government, when they ask us to do small or large scale turn-key privatisation, we have to do it. We do not have any idea about up-grading sweepers' system, it may be beneficial or not. Kolabagan system is good because of Mr Mahbub Ahsan, he does not blackmail and monopolise the system. We could not find such dedicated persons in other areas.

Commentary

- Cost recovery could be a great problem in solid waste management systems.

- This is very true.

Box 29. Key points from brainstorming workshop in Dhaka with sanitary inspectors and supervisors *(continued)*

Narrative

- We are reluctant to start a new system. The primary collection should be under the jurisdiction of city corporation. Privatisation will be imposed in each and every case and we look for alternatives to privatisation. In Dhaka, there is not much of a problem with shortage of sweepers. We pay only Tk 50 per day to daily wage sweepers. A number of sweepers spent a long time in the hope of a permanent job. Sweepers' salaries must be increased, they should be provided with more facilities e.g. more equipment, uniforms. The containers should be picked up every day. We spent about 20 to 22 litres of fuel in every truck.

Commentary

- Policy comes from the top level, often without consultation.

- In Ward No 36 a system similar to Kolabogan area was developed. In Dhanmondi (Ward 49) area, a ward commissioner has made similar vehicles and would like to start a system. In replicating Kolabogan type system, civic system is a major constraint. In low income areas such schemes may not work since the public will not pay. However, in a number of other areas the public does not know about the Kolabagan system.

- Micro-enterprises for low income area is still a challenge.

- Sanitary inspectors know about the innovative schemes.

Annexe 2

Information sources

This section compiles key information sources for the benefit of our readers.

Microenterprise Innovation Project (MIP)

The Microenterprise Innovation Project (MIP) is a U.S. Agency for International Development's (USAID) initiative to support technical and financial assistance, research and training on best practices in microenterprise development and finance. The components of USAID's microenterprise programme are: Microenterprise Best Practices (MBP); Assessing Impact of Microenterprise Services (AIMS); Implementation Grant Program (IGP): Technical Assistance to USAID Missions (MicroServe); and Program for Innovation in Microenterprise (PRIME Fund). MIP's goal is to provide microentrepreneurs, particularly women and the very poor, with greater and more reliable access to financial and business development services to improve enterprise performance and household income. The objective of the MIP is to assist organisations that provide services to the microenterprise sector to increase their capacity, outreach, scale, sustainability, and service quality. For more information:

U.S. Agency for International Development Information Center
Ronald Reagan Building
Washington, D.C. 20523-0016
Telephone: 202-712-4810
Fax: 202-216-3524
Website: http://www.mip.org/

Small Enterprise Development: An International Journal

Small Enterprise Development aims to provide a forum for those involved in the design and administration of small enterprise programmes in developing countries. The journal publishes articles covering all aspects of small enterprise development. For more details, contact:

Intermediate Technology Development Group (ITDG)
103/105 Southampton Row
London WC1B 4HH UK.
Email: journals.edit@itpubs.org.uk
Website: www.oneworld.org/itdg/publications.html

ACCION International

ACCION International is a non-profit organisation that fights poverty through
micro-lending. It is one of the world's leading micro-finance organisations
dedicated to bringing financial services to the smallest of small business
people: street vendors, sandal makers etc. The loans could enable borrowers
to afford basics like running water, better food and schooling for their children. According to ACCION "micro" loans can make the difference between
mere survival and a decent life and with capital, people can develop their
businesses. For more details, contact:

ACCION International
120 Beacon Street
Somerville, MA 02143 USA
Tel: (617) 492-4930
Fax: (617) 876-9509
Email: info@accion.org
Website: http://www.accion.org/

The Foundation for International Community Assistance

The Foundation for International Community Assistance (FINCA), launched
in 1984, now serves more than 80,000 poor families in 14 countries with a
mission to support the economic and human development of families trapped
in severe poverty. It creates "village banks" peer groups of 20 to 50 members,
predominantly women. The village bankers receive three key services:

- Small loans to finance self-employment activities.

- A structured savings plan.

- A community-based system that provides mutual support and encourages
  self-worth.

For more details, contact:

FINCA International, Inc.
1101 14th Street, NW,
11th Floor,
Washington, DC 20005.
Tel: 202 682-1510
Fax: 202 682-1535
Email: finca@villagebanking.org
Website: http://www.villagebanking.org/

UNDP's Micro-finance Project

The goal of a micro-finance project is to create income and employment in poor communities through the development of local microenterprises and, in the process, increase the financial well-being of borrowers, their families, and the community at large. Micro entrepreneurs start rural and urban businesses on a very small scale, usually with no outside assistance. They keep operating costs low by using handmade or second-hand equipment and family labour. Businesses often operate from within the home, so as to make further savings. Unfortunately, those who start and run these businesses have virtually no access to capital beyond sources from family, friends, or professional money-lenders. Moreover, these businesses are largely isolated from one another. Many could build into substantial enterprises, if they had access to productive resources. For more information, contact:

Website: http://www.undp.org/uncdf/sum/Microstart/intro-b.html

Swiss Centre for Development Cooperation in Technology and Management (SKAT)

SKAT is a Swiss consulting firm working internationally in the areas of Water and Sanitation, Architecture and Building, Transport Infrastructure, and Urban Development. SKAT seeks to provide balanced contributions to technical co-operation and to initiate sustainable development processes which empower target groups to achieve self-reliance. SKAT is involved in various projects on micro-enterprise development and recently published:

Involving micro- and small enterprises: Guidelines for municipal managers by Haan Christiaan Hans, Coad A. and Lardinois I. (1998), in collaboration with other agencies. For more information, contact:

SKAT
Swiss Centre for Development Cooperation in Technology and Management,
Vadianstrasse 42,
CH-9000 St.Gallen Switzerland,
Phone:+41 71 228 54 54
Fax: +41 71 228 54 55
Email:info@skat.ch
Website: http://www.skat.ch

WASTE advisers on urban environment and development

WASTE is a multi-disciplinary group of environmental, solid waste management, planning, social development and economic specialists, based in Gouda, the Netherlands. The group acts as a catalyst and a knowledge supplier between experts, sources of information and projects. A network of expertise is constantly maintained and expanded in order to generate appropriate knowledge applicable to situations elsewhere. The emphasis of this network is on low income countries, to stimulate the exchange of experiences among the countries concerned. WASTE provides technological and methodological support and has published various documents on the topic of small and micro-enterprises. For more details, contact:

WASTE Advisers on urban environment and development
Nieuwehaven 201,
2801 CW GOUDA,
The Netherlands.
Tel. +31 (0)182 522625
Fax +31 (0)182 550313
Email: office@waste.nl
Website: http://www.waste.nl

Municipal solid waste management- Involving micro- and small enterprises- Guidelines for municipal managers.
Haan, H.C., Coad, A., and Lardinois, I. 1998. WASTE, GTZ, ILO, SKAT.

This book is about 'micro and small enterprises' (MSEs) and provides tools that can help municipalities to shape the micro- and small-scale enterprises as part of an integrated solid waste management system. This book is targeted at municipal managers, although other professionals such as engineers and administrators who have some responsibility for municipal solid waste management, and who are looking for ways to improve the service or economy will also find this book extremely useful.

Overall, this book is unique as it provides the tools that can help municipalities to shape the MSE component of an integrated solid waste management system.

For more information on how to obtain this book, please see SKAT's information box.

Solid waste management in Latin America
The role of micro-and small enterprises and cooperatives
Moreno, J.A., Ríos, F.R., Lardinois, I.1999. Urban Waste Series 5.
IPES, ACEPESA, WASTE.

The aim of this book is to serve as a guide for introducing effective changes and improvements in solid waste management through explicitly incorporating the experience of micro- and small enterprises and cooperatives (MSE/ Coops), and improving their operation. The key research question presented in this book is how to increase micro-enterprise participation in solid waste management so as to reach the many millions of urban poor throughout the world who are still without proper municipal waste management services. The book is based on research conducted between January and May 1996 in eight cities of Latin American countries: Bolivia, Brazil, Colombia, Costa Rica, El Salvador, Guatemala, Paraguay and Peru. Through the work of ACEPESA, IPES and WASTE, a total of 89 micro-enterprises and cooperatives (MSEs/ Coop) in seven countries were questioned to find out how they are organised, what services they provide, what technology they use, how efficient they are, what their costs are and how costs are covered. The results from the surveys also indicated the types of conditions required to establish successful projects. In general, this book is useful for anyone working or interested in understanding the important role that micro- and small enterprises can provide to communities. This book is also available in Spanish.

This book could be obtained from WASTE (please refer to earlier information box) or
IPES,
Carlos Krundiek 325,
Urbanizacion Santa Catalina,
Lima 13,
Peru.
Email: ipes@mail.cosapidata.com.pe

Non-Governmental Refuse Collection in Low-Income Urban Areas - Lessons Learned From Selected Schemes in Asia, Africa and Latin America.

Pfammatter, R. and Schertenleib, R. 1996. Swiss Federal Institute for Environmental Science and Technology (SANDEC). Department of Water and Sanitation in Developing Countries. (Duebendorf, Switzerland).

This publication summarises some of the experiences gained with non-governmental refuse collection in low-income urban areas through schemes which are operated at the community level by community-based organisations or small private enterprises. The data collected for this publication is based on accumulated visits by or on behalf of SANDEC to selected schemes in different cities in **Asia** (Padang, Cirebon, Yogyakarta, Surabaya, Ujung Padang-Indonesia; Shanghai- China), **Africa** (Ouagadougou- Burkina Faso, Abidjan-Ivory Coast, Accra- Ghana, Douala- Cameroon) and **Latin America** (Cucuta-Colombia, Cajamarca- Peru, Lima-Peru and La Paz- Bolivia).

The publication concludes that small private enterprises and community organisations have a great potential in reducing part of the burden of the responsible public authorities. However, they note that most schemes are still not self-sustainable and face problems which can lead to a breakdown of operation. The main conclusions they draw is the need to focus on:

- collaboration between public authorities and non-governmental actors;

- selection of an affordable and sustainable technology;

- orientation of the users and their involvement in decision-making; and

- assessment and transparent recovery of incurred costs.

In general, this publication is helpful for anyone working or interested in the development of community refuse collection schemes in low-income urban areas. For more details on how to obtain this publication please contact:

EAWAG/SANDEC,
Ueberlandstrasse 133,
CH-8600 Duebendorf,
Switzerland.
Fax: +41-1-823 53 99

Email: hauser@eawag.ch
Website: http://www.sandec.ch/

International Source Book on Environmentally Sound Technologies for Municipal Solid Waste Management.

IETC. 1996. Technical publication series [6], UNEP, Osaka.

This publication is part of the technical publication series sponsored by the United Nations Environmental Programme. The purpose of this book is to provide guidance on issues, experiences and ideas regarding municipal solid waste management (MSWM) from Africa, Asia and the Pacific, Europe, Latin America and the Caribbean, and North America. This work focuses on the similarities across continents. The structure of this book is divided into three sections, namely: a framework for waste management, sound practices and regional overviews and information sources on MSWM. This book's target audience ranges from professionals at the national to the local level. It includes a list of institutions designed to help the readers find organisations that can offer additional information or even assistance in MSWM. This book is useful to use as a source book as it provides a broad overview of technologies and policies for MSWM and offers an initial level of guidance on the choice environmentally sound technologies that are consistent with conditions in developing countries. For more details on how to obtain this publication please contact:

United Nations Environmental Programme (UNEP),
International Environmental Technology Centre (IETC),
2-110 Ryokuchi koen,
Tsurumi-ku,
Osaka 538,
Japan.
Email: hshiroi@unep.org
Website: http://www.unep.or.jp/

Recycling in Asia: Partnerships for responsive solid waste management

United Nations Centre for Regional Development (UNCRD). 1996. Nagoya.

This publication is based on UNCRD research entitled 'Improving solid waste management in the context of metropolitan development and management in the Asian countries'. The research papers presented in this publication are based on a workshop on recycling in South East Asia that focused on the private sector and government, which took place in Makati, Metro Manila, Philippines between the 21st to 23rd of November 1994.

Although this publication is only part of a larger effort being made by various stakeholders directly and indirectly involved in solid waste management, it helps to keep researchers and others interested in this area aware of on-going activities in the field. For more details on how to obtain this publication please contact:

United Nations Centre for Regional Development,
Nagono 1-47-1, Nakamura-ku,
Nagoya 450,
Japan.
Email: rep@uncrd.or.jp
Website: http://www.uncrd.or.jp

Community Businesses - Good practice in urban regeneration
Department of the Environment. London

This publication was commissioned by the Department of the Environment, UK's Inner Cities Directorate between January to May 1988. Community businesses are defined as trading organisations which work for community aims rather than distribution profits. The target audience of this publication is anyone interested in community businesses from groups running projects or for those who may be thinking of establishing one. It could also be useful for those working in a range of fields at the governmental or private level. This book is divided into four sections, namely: the definition and role of community businesses, setting up and running a community business: a guide to best practice, and case studies. Overall this publication does not provide any guidelines as such but rather background information on how a community business can be set up, some best practices and a number of interesting UK based case studies. For more details how to obtain this publication please contact:

HMSO Publications,
PO Box 276, London.
SW8 5DT.